30p

OXFORD PROGRESSIVE ENGLISH READERS

General Editor: D. H. Howe

Gulliver's Travels

Gulliver's Travels

by JONATHAN SWIFT

HONG KONG

OXFORD UNIVERSITY PRESS

KUALA LUMPUR SINGAPORE JAKARTA TOKYO

Oxford University Press, Ely House, London W.I

GLASGOW NEW YORK TORONTO MELBOURNE WELLINGTON
CAPE TOWN IBADAN NAIROBI DAR ES SALAAM LUSAKA ADDIS ABABA
DELHI BOMBAY CALCUTTA MADRAS KARACHI LAHORE DACCA
KUALA LUMPUR SINGAPORE JAKARTA HONG KONG TOKYO

News Building, North Point, Hong Kong

© *Oxford University Press 1973*

Second impression 1974

ISBN 0 19 638256 4

Retold by P.C. Wren

*Simplified according to
the language grading scheme especially compiled by D.H. Howe*

Illustrated by Hanifah Hassan

*Printed by Bright Sun Printing Press Co., Ltd.
5, Yuk Yat Street, Kowloon, Hong Kong*

Contents

Oxford Progressive English Readers Language Scheme

The OPER language grading scheme was especially compiled
by D. H. Howe as a guide to the preparation of language
teaching material for school pupils and adults learning English
as a second or foreign language. The scheme provides lists of
words and language structures subdivided into three grades of
difficulty and meant to be used in conjunction with each other.

The items were chosen according to two main principles: first,
that they are likely to have been learnt or at least encountered
before the stage indicated; second, that they are frequently
occurring and useful, necessary to express a wide range of ideas,
and difficult to replace with simpler words or constructions.

Use of the scheme is intended to eliminate unnecessary
difficulties of language which would otherwise hinder under-
standing and enjoyment.

Part 1
A Voyage to Lilliput

Chapter 1

My father had five sons. I was the third. When I was
fourteen I was sent to the University* of Cambridge.
I studied there for three years. Then my father could
not afford to pay my fees any longer. Therefore I went
to London. I studied with a famous doctor, Mr. James   *5*
Bates. I wanted to be a doctor too and I hoped to
travel abroad later. When I had a little money, I bought
useful books. But Mr. Bates did not pay me very much
so I did not buy many books.

After four years I returned to my home and my   *10*
father. He and some relations gave me £ 40. Also they
promised to send £ 30 each year to me while I learnt
more about medicine. I went to the University of Leyden in Holland for more than two years. I still wanted
to travel so I learnt many things which I could use on   *15*
long voyages.

My first voyages and my marriage
Soon after I returned from Leyden I became a ship's
doctor. Mr. Bates, my old doctor-teacher, advised me to
take this job. For three and a half years I sailed in a ship
called 'Swallow'. I went on voyages to the Levant and   *20*
other places. Then I decided to remain on land, in
London, for a while. Mr. Bates thought this was a good

*university,   place giving degrees and more advanced educa-
tion than secondary schools.

idea this time. He helped me and sent many sick people to see me. I rented a house and later I married Mary Burton. Her father gave her £400 as a wedding present. This was a very useful present indeed.

5   After two years my old friend and helper, Mr. Bates, died. I did not have enough work to do so my wife and friends advised me to travel again.

I learn many new things

This time I sailed to the East Indies several times. My voyages lasted for six years and I earned a satisfactory
10 amount of money. On these journeys I read many good books. Some of them had been written recently while others were written many years before. When I arrived at any port* I watched the foreign people very carefully. I studied their manners and behaviour and I tried to
15 learn their language. My memory is good so I learn new languages easily. Therefore I was quite successful in this.

Once again I became tired of the sea. I planned to stay at home with my wife and family. We moved to a different part of the town near the great River Thames.
20 Ships loaded and unloaded there. I thought that many sailors would need a doctor. But I was unlucky and did not earn enough money for my family. Therefore I accepted a good job on the 'Antelope'. This ship was voyaging to the South Sea Islands.

Another voyage and a great storm

25 We sailed from Bristol on 4 May 1699. At first the weather was good. Then a great storm drove us to the north of Van Diemen's Land. This storm lasted a long, long time. Twelve sailors died from over-work and hard conditions. The rest were very weak.

*port,   a town with a harbour.

November 5 was the beginning of summer in that part
of the world. The weather was dull and cloudy. Suddenly the sailors saw a rock close to the ship. The wind
blew strongly. The captain did his best to steer away
from this rock but we hit it. There was shouting and dis-   5
order. Our ship was badly damaged and we started to
sink quickly. Six sailors and I managed to lower a boat
before the 'Antelope' sank into the sea. We moved away
from that dangerous rock and rowed for several miles.
But we lost our strength. We could not row any more   10
and we floated without aim or direction.

Saved from drowning
   The wind suddenly hit our boat. We were thrown in
the sea. I never saw any of my companions again. I
swam and swam with some help from the wind and the
waves. I allowed my legs to drop sometimes but I could   15
not touch the bottom. I wanted to stop and rest because I was so tired. I was ready to stop swimming. I
was almost drowning when my feet touched land!
   The water grew shallower. I walked for about a mile
before I got to the shore. When I reached dry land it   20
was about eight o'clock in the evening. I could not see
any people or houses and I was too weak and tired to
look for any. The grass on the beach was the shortest
and softest I had ever seen. I lay down on it. I was so
hungry and tired that I felt half-dead. I fell asleep at   25
once and I slept very well for nine hours.

I am a prisoner
   When I awoke I tried to get up. I could not move.
My arms and legs were fastened to the ground. My long
thick hair was fastened down also. There were several
thin pieces of string across my body from my shoulders   30

to the top of my legs. I could not move anything except my eyes. The sun soon became hot and bright. The bright sun hurt my eyes so I closed them.

I could hear a lot of noise around me. Many things
5 were moving too but I could not see anything except the sky.

After a time I felt something on my left leg. It was alive and it moved very gently over my body towards my chin. I turned my eyes down as far as I could. Then
10 I saw a tiny man, only six inches tall. He carried a bow and arrow* in his hand with more arrows in a bag on his back. At the same time I felt about forty more little things climbing over me.

*arrow,   a thin pointed stick
to be shot with a bow.

I try to get free

This was the biggest surprise of my life. I roared so loudly that all the tiny men ran away. They were very frightened. Many jumped to the ground. Some of them were hurt quite badly when they fell over my body. Soon these little men came back. One of them came 5 very close as he wanted to see my whole face. He lifted up his hands and eyes to show that I pleased him very much. Then he cried out in a high and clear voice. I could not understand his language. The others repeated his words. I did not know then what they were saying. 10

All this time I was lying there in a very uncomfortable manner. I tried hard to get free. I managed to break some of the strings. Then I twisted some pieces of wood out of the ground. My left arm was free! At the same time I pulled hard on the left side of my head. It was very painful but I loosened some of the bindings there. Now I was able to move my head about two inches.

As I was doing this the little people ran away. I did
5 not have time to catch hold of even one of them. I heard someone shout an order in a loud voice. At once about one hundred arrows were shot into my left side. These felt like sharp needles and were very painful. Some hit my face and I shouted with pain. I covered my
10 face with my left hand and I tried to break all the strings now. I wanted to get free but the little men shot more arrows at me. Some tried to push their spears* into me also.

A small man speaks to Gulliver

Luckily I was wearing a leather jacket and their spears
15 were not sharp enough to go through. I decided to lie still until night-time. My left hand was not tied so I thought it would be easy to get free. As soon as it was dark I would be able to get away. When I was standing up I was certain that I could defeat my guards.
20 But my plan was not needed.

The little men saw that I was lying still. They did not shoot any more arrows but four yards from my head there was a sound of knocking. My head could turn a little way and I saw that they were building a platform
25 about eighteen inches from the ground. Four people were standing on it. One of them began to make a speech. He was taller than his companions and he seemed more important too.

I could not understand any of his words. Sometimes
30 his voice sounded kind. Sometimes he sounded angry.

*spear,   a long stick with a metal point at one end. It is used for fighting.

All this time I was in pain because it was so hot. I lifted my hand to protect my face from the sun. Then I pointed to my open mouth because I was hungry. The man who had been speaking understood my signs.

I am given food and drink

He left the platform and ordered some people to 5
place ladders against my sides. They did this at once.
More than a hundred men climbed up the ladders. They
carried baskets of meat which their king had sent for
me. The meat in each basket came from a different animal. I did not know the names of these animals at all. 10
There were many different shapes but each piece was
smaller than the wings of a bird.

I ate two or three pieces in one mouthful. Their
loaves of bread were as small as peas. I ate them three
at a time and they fed me as fast as they could. Then I 15
showed that I was thirsty. They thought about this for
a little time. Then someone had a clever idea. They
rolled a barrel* close to my head and they knocked off
its top. I lifted up my head a little and I opened my
mouth. It was not water in the barrel. Still, I emptied it 20
with one big swallow. The barrel held about half a pint
of wine which had a pleasant taste. The little men
rushed up with another barrel. I emptied that very
quickly as I was so thirsty. Then I moved my head to
ask for another. But there was no more. I had drunk all 25
their wine! The little people were very pleased because
I had eaten their food. They shouted and danced up and
down on my body. Next they asked me to throw down
the empty barrels. Everybody moved out of the way. I
threw with my left hand and once more everyone 30

*barrel,   round box usually made from wood with flat ends
and round sides.

shouted with joy and surprise. Secretly I wanted to throw down forty or fifty men also. But I did not do this as they had been so kind to me. Also I remembered the pain from their pointed arrows.

I remain a prisoner

5   These men were very brave as I was a monster* to them. They walked all over me and they were not afraid.

The Emperor* of this strange country sent one of his gentlemen to see me. He wished to talk to me as soon as
10 I had finished my meal. He climbed first upon my ankle. He moved along my body with twelve men behind him. In his hand he was carrying orders from the Emperor. When this gentleman reached my face he made a long speech. He waved his papers and pointed his fingers. I
15 understood that he was showing me the way to the capital city.

I answered quickly but nobody understood my words. I pointed to the strings round my body. I wanted him to untie them. But he shook his head. He placed his
20 own hands and feet together to show that I was a prisoner. He pretended to eat and to drink. This puzzled me and then I understood. I could have food but I could not have freedom.

This made me angry. I tried to break the thin ropes
25 and string. Immediately hundreds of arrows were fired at me. My hands were soon full of arrows and they felt very sore. I lay still and decided not to struggle again. I was truly a prisoner.

Many people now came to look at me. My ropes were
30 loosened a little and I turned to my right side. They

*monster,   over-large animal, plant or person.
*emperor,   a great and powerful king.

tried to be kind for they rubbed some sweet oil on my hands. Later I went to sleep for about eight hours. I slept for such a long time because there was some sleeping medicine in the wine I had drunk. The Emperor had ordered this to be given to me. 5

The Emperor's plan for me

I found out later that he had planned everything. His people had told him about the monster they had found in the grass. He had ordered that I must be tied down. He had sent the food and wine with the sleeping medicine in it. Now the citizens were making a machine to 10 carry me to the capital.

These men were very clever at doing sums. They were very good engineers* too. They used machines with wheels to carry long heavy goods. They built their ships in the forests where there was plenty of wood. Then the 15 machines carried these ships to the sea. The planned to build the strongest and biggest machine in his kingdom to carry me.

Four hundred wood-workers and engineers started their work. After some time they had made a platform 20 about seven feet long and four feet wide. It was three inches from the ground and it had twenty-two wheels.

It was placed next to me. These tiny men planned to lift me on that platform. All this time I remained fast asleep. 25

Moving to the city

Eighty sticks, each twelve inches long, were fixed in the ground. The workmen fastened strong thin ropes round my neck, body, arms and legs. Nine hundred of

*engineer,   person who plans bridges, machines, factories etc.

the Emperor's strongest men pulled these ropes which
went round wheels on the sticks. They pulled and pulled
for about three hours. First I was lifted up a little. Then
I was dropped carefully until I was lying on the top of
5 the wooden platform. All this time I was fast asleep.

One thousand five hundred horses all about four and
a half inches high, began to pull the machine to the
capital. It was half a mile away. When we had been
travelling for about four hours I woke up. However, I
10 was awakened in a very strange way.

Something went wrong with the platform so the
horses were stopped. Some young men wanted to watch
me when I was sleeping. They climbed on my body and
then on my face. One of them, an officer in the army,
15 put his spear in my nose. I sneezed loudly and woke up.
The young men disappeared quickly and quietly. About
three weeks later I discovered why I had woken up so
suddenly. I was also told about this journey for I was
asleep when it happened.

20 When the machine was mended we set off again. We
marched all day and rested at night. Five hundred
guards were standing round me. Half of them were
holding torches. The other half were ready to shoot
their bows and arrows if I moved. The next morning, as
25 soon as it was daylight, we started marching and pulling
again. I was still lying on the wooden platform. At midday we arrived at the city and we stopped about two
hundred yards from the city's entrance.

My new house

The Emperor, with all his followers, came out to
30 meet us. But a group of important officers would not allow the Emperor to climb over me. They said that I was

too dangerous. There was a large temple* close to us. Many years ago someone was cruelly killed there so all the religious pictures and furniture had been taken away. I was pulled inside this building. Its chief door was four feet high and two feet wide so I could creep 5 easily through it. On each side of the door there was a small window, about six inches from the ground. The Emperor sent a workman with ninety-one iron chains. He climbed through the window and locked these chains to my leg. Thirty-six special locks were needed to fasten 10 these chains.

On the other side of the road and opposite the temple, there was a tall narrow building. It was five feet high. The Emperor and his servants climbed up there to look at me. About one hundred thousand people also 15 came from the city to see me. I think that ten thousand climbed over my body. The guards tried to stop them but it was impossible. Then an order came from the Emperor. Anyone who climbed over me would die.

The workmen noticed that I could not break the 20 chains so they cut off all the other strings round me. I sat up. Then I stood up. This surprised everyone very much but I was sad for I was still a prisoner.

The chains were about six feet long. They were fastened to my left leg so I could move for about half a 25 circle. I managed to creep inside the temple and there I was able to lie down at full length.

*temple,   building used for religious purposes.

Chapter 2

When I stood up I could see the beautiful country all around me. The fields, about twelve yards square, were like flower gardens to me. The tallest trees in the forest were a foot taller than I was. The town looked like a
5 painted picture.

The Emperor came down from the tall building where he had been watching me. He rode towards me but his horse was very frightened. It jumped up on its back legs. The Emperor was a very good rider and did not fall.
10 Then his followers held the horse until it was quiet and the Emperor got down.

He walked round and round me but he stayed at a safe distance! He ordered food and drink. His cooks and servants brought these in boxes which they could push
15 along. I emptied twenty boxes which were filled with food and ten filled with drink. Each box held only two or three mouthfuls.

The Emperor and his family

The Empress,* and the young princes and princesses sat on chairs a short distance away from me. When the
20 Emperor got down from his horse, they came and joined him.

The Emperor was taller than any of his officers. That means that he was taller by the breadth of my nail. His face was strong and manly, his body was straight and he
25 moved in a light and easy way. At this time he was twenty-eight years old. In this country he was thought to be quite old. For the past seven years he had ruled

*empress, a woman who rules or the wife of an emperor.

happily and well. I lay flat on the ground so that I could
see him better. Afterwards he often stood on my hand
so I know now that I described him correctly.

His clothes were very plain and simple. They looked
half-Asian and half-European. He also wore a gold hat to   5
protect his head. This hat had beautiful feathers and
jewels on it. He held his sword in his hand so that he
could defend himself if I broke my chains. This sword
was three inches long and the gold top was covered with
diamonds.   10

We have language difficulties

The Emperor spoke in a high voice but I could hear
all the words clearly. His followers and all the ladies
wore rich and beautiful clothes. The ground where they
were standing looked like gold and silver cloth.

His Majesty* and I often spoke to each other but   15
neither of us understood a single word. I tried words
from many languages — Dutch, French, Spanish, Italian
and Latin. No one could understand my words, not even
the cleverest of the Emperor's followers.

After about two hours the Emperor left. His wife,   20
children and their servants went also. There were strong
guards around me. This was to stop the crowd of people
from hurting and annoying me. One or two shot their
arrows however, and one arrow just missed my eye.

An act of kindness

An officer told the guards to hold six men who had   25
been annoying me. These men were given to me and I
had to choose their punishment. I put five of them in
my pocket. Then I pretended to eat the sixth man.

*Majesty,   used when speaking to a king, queen, emperor or
             empress.

The poor man screamed terribly. The guards were worried when they saw my knife in my hand. Was I going to cut up the man? But I only cut the binding round his hands. Then I put him on his feet and I let
5   him go. I lifted the other five men out of my pocket and put them gently on the ground too.

The people and the soldiers were very pleased with my great kindness. They told the Emperor about it immediately.

10   At night I crept inside the temple. I lay down on the hard ground to go to sleep. Two weeks later, these people had made a bed for me. They had joined six hundred of their little beds together to make one bed for me.

The Emperor asks for advice

The news of my arrival spread through the country.
15   Everybody wanted to see me and the villages became empty. The farms needed the farmers so the Emperor ordered his people to return to their homes. If people wished to stand near the temple, they were ordered to pay a fee.

20   At the same time the Emperor asked all his advisers for their advice about me. They were very worried. If I broke my chains I might be dangerous. I was eating so much food that soon all the people would be very hungry. The farmers could not grow enough food to feed all
25   of us.

The wise men thought that they should kill me. But they would not be able to bury me. My dead body would smell. This might cause much illness all over the country.

My kindness is rewarded

30   While the advisers were talking together, an officer

arrived. He told the Emperor about my kindness to the six men. This pleased him very much. He ordered all the villagers near the capital to take food to me. Every morning they brought six cows, forty sheep, bread, wine and other necessary things. The Emperor ordered his *5* officers to make notes about all this food. Later the villagers were paid for it by an officer who looked after all the money in the kingdom.

I was given six hundred servants and they lived in tents near me. Three hundred tailors made some clothes *10* for me. They were the same kind as everyone else was wearing in that country. Six of the greatest teachers taught me their language.

The horses that belonged to the Emperor, his soldiers and noblemen* did their exercises near me. The Em- *15* peror ordered this so that the horses would not be frightened when they saw me.

I study the language

After about three weeks, I knew some of the language. The Emperor often visited me to see how I was getting and he taught me himself. I learnt to say the *20* words 'please set me free'. I repeated them to him every day. He always replied something like this. 'I cannot do this at present. You must promise that you will not make war in my country. We will look after you well. We hope you will do your best to become our true *25* friend.'

He wanted his officers to see if I was carrying any dangerous things.

'I will take off all my clothes for you immediately,' I said. 'You can examine all my pockets also.' *30*

*noble(man),   a person of high birth.

Two officers examine my pockets

'The law says that two officers must do this,' the Emperor replied. 'They cannot look easily at your clothes without your permission. Please help them and do not hurt them. If the officers take anything away

5   they will return it when you leave this country. Or you will be paid for it.'

Two officers came up to me. I lifted them up and I placed them in my coat pockets. Then I moved them into all my other pockets. But I did not show them a

10   special secret one. I kept my watch, my money and one or two other things in this pocket. I did not want to hand these things in.

The two men wrote down on a sheet of paper the names of what they found in my pockets. They gave

15   this to the Emperor and this is what the paper contained.

The things found in my pockets

'In the left pocket we found a big silver box. We asked the Man-Mountain to open this. There was a lot of dust inside. We stepped inside the box and this dust

20   made us sneeze and sneeze. (This was my snuff* box.)

'In another pocket there were a lot of white sheets which were as big as three men. They were folded over many times and they were tied together with a thick rope. There were many letters on these sheets. Each

25   letter was half as big as the palm of our hands. (A few envelopes with letters inside them.)

'We found a kind of engine. It had about twenty long sticks on the back which looked like the railings round Your Majesty's garden. We think this must be the Man-

30   Mountain's comb.

*snuff,   tobacco leaves which have been dried and made into a powder to be taken in the nose.

'In the right pocket of his leg-clothes (they did not know the word for trousers) we saw a piece of iron. This was about the same height as one of us and there was a hole in it. There were two pieces of iron fixed on
5   this. Then the whole piece of iron was fastened to a piece of wood. We do not know how to use this engine. There is another in the left pocket. (These were my guns.)

My knives, watch and money

'In the same pockets we found great flat pieces of
10   metal. Some were white and some were yellow and there were different sizes of them. They were very heavy and we could not lift them easily. There were also two black things. We could not reach the top of them. But we could see that they held flat pieces of steel. The
15   man told us that he used one to cut his meat. He used the other to cut the hair on his face.

'From one front pocket a line of silver rings was hanging, with a wonderful engine at the bottom. It looked like a flat ball. Half of it was made from silver
20   and the other half was made from a strange water-coloured metal. We could see right through this half. The machine made a noise like the beat of a heart. We think that perhaps it contains an animal or a god in his religion. We think it holds a god for the man looks at
25   this machine before he does anything. It seems to show him when to do anything. In the opposite pocket there was a big bag. It was filled with large pieces of yellow metal. This man must be very rich if these pieces are made from gold.

My sword and guns

30   'Round his waist this man was wearing a belt made

from the skin of a big animal. A sword was hanging on this belt. The sword was as big as five tall men. We found another bag hanging from the belt. It was divided into two parts, each big enough to hold three or four men. We found very heavy metal circles in one part, as big as a man's head. In the other we found black powder. (These were for my guns.)

'This is exactly what we found on the Man-Mountain's body. He was very polite as he knew that we were Your Majesty's officers.'

When all this was read aloud to His Majesty he asked me gently to give in all these things.

First he called for my sword.

The Emperor shows interest

At the same time he ordered some of his soldiers to gather round. Their bows and arrows were ready to fire at me. He asked me to take out my sword. The seawater had not spoilt it very much and most of it was very bright. I waved it around and the soldiers shouted loudly. They were surprised as well as frightened because my sword was shining like fire in the sunshine.

The Emperor, who was a very brave man, was not so frightened. He told me to put away my sword in its cover. This I did and then I placed it on the ground.

Next he asked for 'the iron with a hole in it'. He wanted my gun. I pulled it out of my pocket and I tried to explain how to use it. I offered to shoot something with my gun. His Majesty agreed to this. I told him not to be frightened. Then I pointed the gun to the sky and there was a loud bang. Hundreds of people fell down as though they were dead. The Emperor did not fall over but he was not very calm for quite a long time.

I placed my guns with my sword and I gave them my

bag of gun-powder and bullets.* I did not know all the
correct words to use but I asked the soldiers to be careful with the gun-powder. If a flame touched it then the
powder would destroy the whole palace.*

The Emperor examines my watch

5   The Emperor was very interested in my watch. He
ordered two guards to carry it to him. They hung the
watch on a thick piece of wood. Then they carried this
on their shoulders. He was filled with surprise at the
noise which never stopped. He liked to watch the
10   minute-hand. He could watch this while it moved for his
eyes were much sharper than mine.
     He asked all his wise men what they thought about
my watch. They gave him many different and strange
answers.
15   I showed the Emperor my silver and copper money
and my purse with nine gold pieces in it. He examined
my knife, my razor,* comb, snuff-box, handkerchief
and letters. He returned everything to me except the
sword, guns and gun-powder. These were taken to His
20   Majesty's store-house.

*bullet,   a piece of metal to be fired from a gun.

*palace,   house of a king or emperor.

*razor,   a knife for cutting hair on the chin.

Chapter 3

My gentle ways and good behaviour pleased the Emperor, the men who lived in the palace, the army and all the people who lived in that country. Therefore I hoped that I should get my freedom, soon. Slowly everyone lost their fear of me. I tried to be kind and friendly all the time. 5

Sometimes five or six villagers danced on my head. The boys and girls played games by hiding themselves in my hair.

I asked many times for my freedom. His Majesty 10 spoke to his advisers about this. Everyone agreed to set me free except the Emperor's Admiral.* He hated me. I did not know why.

At last he too agreed with all the rest. He came himself to see me with several important officers. This is 15 what he told me to do. I had to hold my right foot in my left hand. I next put the middle finger of my right hand on the top of my head and my thumb on the tip of my right ear. Then I had to promise many things very seriously. 20

I make many promises
These were the promises.

First: The Man-Mountain must not leave the Kingdom without permission.

Second: He must not enter our capital city without an order from the Emperor. He must tell the people 25 about this two hours earlier. Then they can remain at home in safety.

*admiral,   a high officer in the navy.

Third: The Man-Mountain must use the chief roads. He must not lie down on the grass or in the fields of corn.

Fourth: He must be very careful when he goes for a
5 walk. He must not step on anybody, or on any horses or carriages.* He must not lift up any citizens without their permission.

Fifth: If the Emperor wishes to send a message to someone quickly, the Man-Mountain must help him. He
10 must carry the messenger and his horse in his pocket for a journey of six days. Then he must bring back the messenger safely. And he must do this once each month.

Sixth: He must help us against our enemies in the island of Blefuscu. He must help to destroy all their
15 ships. We know that these ships are getting ready to attack us now.

Seventh: The Man-Mountain must help our workmen to lift some heavy stones. These are needed for walls in the city park.
20 Eighth: He must walk all round our lands in two months' time. He must count his steps and then he can tell us the exact distance round our country.

Lastly: If he promises to do all these things, the Man-Mountain will be given food for 1,724 people. He can
25 visit the Emperor when he wants to. The Emperor promises to help him in many ways.

I am free at last

I agreed to everything though I did not like some of the promises. The Admiral still did not like me and he made everything difficult for me. The Emperor himself
30 watched when my chains were unlocked. I was free at last. I bowed politely to him and thanked him.

*_carriage_,   vehicle used for carrying people, generally pulled
            by horses.

'I hope you will be a useful servant of the kingdom of Lilliput,' the Emperor said. 'I hope you will deserve my kindness now and in the future.'

Each day I now received as much food as 1,724 people of Lilliput could eat. I asked someone how they had   *5* worked out this number. He told me that the Emperor's doctors had measured my height. I was twelve times taller than anyone else there. So my body contained 1,724 times as much as theirs. Therefore the doctors had decided that I needed 1,724 times more food!   *10*

Chapter 4

I wanted to see the capital city of Lilliput, Milendo,
very much. I asked for permission to visit it after I was
set free. The Emperor agreed immediately. I promised
not to hurt the people or their houses. Everyone was
5 told about my visit and they were advised to remain in-
doors until I had left.

There was a big wall all round Milendo, two and a
half feet high and one foot across. Every ten feet along
this wall an extra tall building had been built. I stepped
10 over the great west entrance and I walked very slowly
and gently through the chief streets. I did not wear my
coat as it was so long. It might damage the roofs of the
houses while I walked along. Big crowds watched me
from windows and roof-tops. Some of the houses had
15 five floors each.

Milendo appeared to be the busiest city that I had
ever seen. It is built in an exact square and each city
wall is five hundred feet long. The chief streets divide
it into quarters. These streets are five feet wide. There
20 are many lanes as well but these are only twelve to
eighteen inches wide. There seemed to be many good
shops and markets for the five hundred thousand
citizens.

The Emperor's palace

The Emperor's palace is in the centre of the city at
25 the spot where the two great streets meet. His Majesty
gave me permission to step over the palace wall. The
first building inside the wall is square, and forty feet
in area. I could see two more buildings inside the first

square. I was told that the inside building, that is the
third one, contained the rooms of the Emperor and all
his family.

I wanted to see these rooms very much but it was
5 very difficult to do this. The entrance from one square
to another was only eighteen inches high and seven
inches wide. The outer buildings were five feet high. I
could not step over them, however, for I would have
damaged them very much. The Emperor was dis-
10 appointed at this for he wanted me to see his beautiful
home.

I have a plan

After some time, I thought of a plan. I cut down
some of the largest trees in the park outside the city.
Then I made two stools about three feet high. They
15 were strong and I could stand on them. I went to Milendo again. All the people remained inside their houses
again and I went to the palace with my two stools.
When I reached the outer building I stood on one stool.
Next I lifted the second stool over the roof and put it
20 down between the outer wall and the next building. It
was eight feet wide here. Then I stepped from one stool
to the other. I pulled up the first stool with a curved
stick and I put it down between the second and third
building. I stepped over again and in front of me there
25 was the Emperor's palace.

The windows were wide open. I had to lie sideways
to look inside. The rooms were very beautiful and I
could see the Empress and her children. The Empress
smiled and she put her hand out of the window. I kissed
30 it because I wished to greet her politely and correctly. I
returned shortly afterwards to the temple.

This temple was now my home and not my prison.

The Emperor asks for help

About two weeks later, a very important officer of the king visited me. He wanted to talk to me seriously about something in the kingdom.

I offered to lie down so that I could hear all his words. But he asked me to hold him in my hand instead. 5
This I did. He told me that, very soon, there would be a war between Lilliput and the nearby country of Blefuscu. The Emperor feared the navy* of Blefuscu very much. It was large and strong. Even now, it was getting ready to attack Lilliput's shores. 10

'His Majesty places his hopes in you,' the officer said. 'He ordered me to tell you all this. He wishes you to be ready to help him and the country in any way.'

'Please tell His Majesty,' I replied, 'that I will do anything I can. I am willing to risk my own life to fight the 15
enemies of the Emperor and his kingdom.'

*navy, warships; officers and men who work on warships.

Chapter 5

I discovered that Blefuscu was an island. It was north-
east of Lilliput and the water between them was only
eight hundred yards wide. No one in Blefuscu knew anything about me for they had not seen me. They were
5 not allowed to speak to anyone in Lilliput either.

I told His Majesty that I was thinking of a plan to
take all the ships of the enemy at once. These ships were
in their harbour waiting for a good wind. I asked the
most skilled Lilliputian sailor about the depth of the sea
10 between the two shores.

'About six feet in the middle and four feet at the
sides,' he said at once.

I walked almost to the coast* and hid behind a hill
there. I pulled out a special glass from my secret pocket.
15 This could make faraway things look very close and it
meant that I could see all the ships of the enemy. There
were about fifty war-ships and a number of ships to
carry soldiers.

I reach the enemy's ships

I returned to my house. I ordered bars of iron and
20 thick strong wire to be brought to me. The wire was
only as thick as thread so I used three lengths to make
a rope. I twisted three iron bars to make one hook and
altogether I made fifty hooks and fifty ropes. I fastened
one hook to each rope, then I went back to the coast.
25 I walked out into the sea as far as I could and then I
began to swim. Less than half an hour later I reached
the enemy ships.

*coast,   land near or by the edge of the sea.

I stood up. The enemy were so frightened that they jumped out of their ships and swam to the shore. I fastened a hook to each ship and I tied all the ropes together at the other end.

While I was doing this, the people of Blefuscu shot *5* thousands of arrows at me. Many arrows stuck in my hands and face. These were very painful and I could not work quite as quickly after that. Luckily I was wearing my glasses. These protected my eyes against the arrows.

As soon as I had fastened all the hooks into the ships *10* I held the knot at the other end of the ropes. I pulled and I pulled.

The enemy lose their ships

Nothing happened! The ships were fastened to iron hooks at the bottom of the sea. These hooks were at the other end of the ships. I could not move any of the *15* ships though I pulled very hard. So I decided to break the ropes which held these strong hooks. This was very dangerous and difficult.

I walked round to the other end of the ships and about two hundred arrows went into my hands and *20* face. The rest of my body was covered by the sea-water. I broke the threads then I went back to the front of the ships. I held the knot which fastened the fifty ropes and pulled once more. This time all the enemy ships came sailing along. I half-swam and half-walked back to *25* Lilliput.

The people of Blefuscu were dumb were surprise at first. They thought I was going to sink their ships or send them away. Suddenly they understood what I was doing. They saw that the Blefuscu ships were all going *30* to Lilliput so they began to scream and shout. I cannot describe the terrible sounds I heard.

The Emperor rewards me

I stopped to pull out the arrows from my face and I came safely back to Lilliput. The Emperor and all his followers were waiting on the shore. They saw the enemy ships moving forward in a half-moon shape. But where was the Man-Mountain? Were these the enemy ships coming nearer and nearer? The Emperor was truly frightened.

Shortly afterwards, everyone could see me. When the water was shallow enough I held up the end of the ropes to which the ships were fastened.

'Long live the Emperor of Lilliput,' I shouted.

When I was standing on dry land the Emperor thanked me over and over again. He rewarded me by giving me the name 'Lord'.* This was the highest reward in the kingdom.

I anger the Emperor

Next he asked me to bring across the sea any Blefuscu ships that I could find. He now wanted to make Blefuscu a part of Lilliput. I did not wish to hurt the people of Blefuscu any more so I refused very politely. His Majesty never forgave me for this. He forgot that I had saved his country for him. He forgot that I had brought all the Blefuscu navy to him. He was angry because he wished me to destroy the enemy completely. His anger was so great that it almost caused my death a little later on.

About three weeks later, messengers from Blefuscu asked for peace. The peace conditions gave many advantages to the Emperor and to Lilliput. The Emperor remained very unfriendly towards me. He showed clearly by his actions that I was not his favourite any more.

*lord,   name given to a nobleman.

However, I had another chance to help a little later. I thought that the Emperor would be very pleased with me after this.

A serious fire

One night I heard the cries of many people at my
5   door. They were shouting the word 'Fire' over and over again. Several of the Emperor's servants asked me to hurry to the palace. The room belonging to the Empress was on fire.

I got up immediately. The moon was shining so I
10   could see clearly. I was very careful and did not touch anyone on my way to the palace.

All the people were passing buckets of water from hand to hand. I threw this water on the fire for them. But this was very slow for they had to carry the water
15   a long way. Each bucket was the size of my finger-nail. The flames were growing higher. We could not put them out. It seemed hopeless. The beautiful palace would be destroyed in front of me. Then I had an idea.

How the fire was put out

I ran towards the water. I knelt down and filled my
20   mouth with it. Then I spat this water over the fire. It was not very nice but it was the only thing I could do at the time. It was successful and in three minutes the fire was completely out. The lovely building was safe.

It was daylight by this time. I did not wait to see the
25   Emperor for a very good reason. Spitting was not allowed near the palace. Any person who did this would die. This was the law for everybody.

His Majesty sent me a message. He said that he was ordering the Chief Judge to sign a pardon for me. But
30   this pardon did not come. The Empress hated the way in

which I had saved her rooms. She would not live in them again. I knew therefore that she would cause trouble for me.

Chapter 6

In the kingdom of Lilliput there are many interesting laws and customs.* Punishments are very cruel. Everyone there loves peace and order. They would tear to pieces anyone who hurts an official.*

5   But the law also protects the helpless. It punishes anyone who wants to cause unnecessary trouble. It says that most men can protect their goods from thieves. But many cannot protect themselves against wicked people who will cheat and rob them. The punishment for
10 cheating in Lilliput is death.

    Once I tried to help a man. He had stolen a lot of money from his master yet I asked the Emperor to forgive him. The Emperor was very surprised. The man had done something wrong therefore he must be punished.
15 I explained that the customs in my country were different. Sometimes a second chance was given to a thief. But the Emperor was not pleased.

The laws of Lilliput

    In Lilliput men receive a reward if they keep all the laws for seventy-three months. They are given some
20 money and they can add the word 'legal'* to their name. They thought my customs and laws were not good as I told them we have punishments but we do not have rewards which are given through the law. They showed me their statue of Justice.* She has six eyes.
25 Two in front, two behind and one on each side. This

*custom,   usual behaviour in a group of people.
*official,   person with a high job in a government or with a king.
*legal,   working with the law.
*Justice,   acting in a fair and right way.

means that Justice is able to look all round her. She
holds a bag of gold in her right hand. This is to reward
good people. But she carries a sword in her left hand.
This is to punish wicked people.

Good behaviour is very important in this country. 5
When a man is looking for work his behaviour is more
important than his ability. It is believed that a well-
behaved man will be able to do any kind of work. If he
happens to make a mistake, it will be an honest mistake. It will not hurt anybody. But a clever yet badly- 10
behaved man will be a danger to everybody.

The Emperors of Lilliput say that they are acting for
God. Anyone who does not believe in their God is not
allowed to work for the Government.

Men must show thankfulness to those who have 15
helped them. The punishment for being ungrateful may
be death. They say that if a man does not love the one
who has helped him, then he cannot love other people
either.

The children of Lilliput

The people of Lilliput have a strange idea about chil- 20
dren. They say that children do not ask to be born.
Therefore children do not belong to their parents. They
belong to Lilliput. When children are twenty months old
they leave their parents. They go to homes which are
only used for babies and children. There they are looked 25
after by special nurses and teachers.

It is said here that parents do not really want their
children. Parents cannot care for them properly as there
is so much trouble in the world. These special schools
can look after children in the correct way. 30

In these special schools, children are taught how to
be honest and to think carefully. They do not study to

pass examinations. Instead, they learn all about how to be good and they learn to love their country. There are separate schools for the children of noblemen and for the children of working people. The girls and boys
5   are in different schools or homes.

The baby nobles wear simple clothes and eat plain food. Men dress them until they are four years old. After that time, they dress themselves. Even the princes dress themselves. They are not allowed to talk to the
10 servants. They must play with each other and a teacher remains with them all the time.

How the children are brought up
The parents of the children are allowed to see them twice a year. They may kiss their child when they first see him and again when they are leaving. But a teacher
15 stands near by to see that the parents do not bring any toys or sweets. The parents may not even whisper any sweet or loving words.

The Emperor's officials decide how much money each family must pay to the school. Children of nobles
20 remain at school until they are fifteen. The schools for other boys are almost the same. But they leave school when they are eleven years old. Then they begin to learn about their future work.

The schools for daughters of high birth are almost
25 the same as the schools for sons. Women servants dress the girls until they are five. The girls are taught to be brave and wise. They must be equal to men when they are grown up. They learn to be useful, helpful and wise companions to their future husbands.
30 The girls return to their homes when they are ready for marriage. This is when they are about twenty-one. Their parents are usually very grateful to the teachers

for all their care and kindness. The daughters from poor families are taught to do useful work. They learn to become wives too.

There are no beggars in Lilliput. Old people and people who are ill go to the hospitals. These are all free.   *5*

Clothes are made for me

I remained in Lilliput for nine months and thirteen days. I like to use my hands so I made a table and a chair. I used trees from the royal park for them. Two hundred women-tailors made me some shirts, bedsheets and table-cloths. They used the strongest cloth *10* they could find but it was very thin. Therefore they sewed three pieces together to make each thing.

The tailors measured me when I was lying on the ground. One stood on my neck, another stood on my waist. They held a piece of string between them. A third *15* woman measured the length of the string. Her ruler was one inch long. They also measured my old shirt. When they had finished the measuring and the sewing, the new shirt fitted me exactly.

Three hundred men-tailors made some other clothes *20* for me. This time I knelt down to be measured. A tailor let down a piece of string from my neck to the ground. This was the length of my coat. I measured my sleeves and waist myself. My clothes were made in my house for the other houses were too small. When my clothes *25* were finished they looked very unusual because the cloth was cut in many different shapes and sizes.

Lilliput cannot afford to feed me

Three hundred men cooked my food. They lived with their families in little huts near my house. Each man cooked two dishes a day. I used to lift up twenty *30*

servants in my hand and put them on my table. A hundred more worked on the ground. Some carried the dishes of food while others carried the barrels of wine. The servants who were standing on the table pulled up all these things. One dish of their meat was equal to one *5* mouthful for me. A barrel gave me a single drink.

One day His Majesty came to watch me while I ate. He was surprised to see that I could put twenty or thirty chickens on the end of my knife. I could eat big birds in a single mouthful. *10*

But something bad happened. It was the result of the Emperor's visit to me. My enemy, the Admiral, said the cost of my food was too high. Lilliput could not afford to pay for it. They could not afford to keep me alive.

Just after this time, I made a great mistake. I ad- *15* mitted that I wished to visit the country of Blefuscu.

Chapter 7

I do not know very much about Kings and their followers. I had only heard stories about wicked noblemen
in Europe. I did not expect to find any in Lilliput. But
it seemed that some people were making a secret plan
5 against me. This is how I discovered it.

I was getting ready to make a trip to Blefuscu. One
night one of the Emperor's officers came to visit me
secretly. I had helped him once and he was grateful to
me. He did not want anyone to notice him and he would
10 not tell my servant his name. He said that he must see
me. I understood what he meant. At once I lifted him
up and put him in my pocket. Then I fastened the door.
I told my servant to say that I was ill and that I had
gone to sleep. I did not want to see anyone else that
15 night.

I put my visitor on the table. We greeted each other
but he was very worried. He asked me to listen to him
patiently.

'Several secret meetings have been held,' he said. 'The
20 Admiral has always hated you. The Emperor is angry
with you because you would not destroy all the ships of
Blefuscu. Now the Emperor is afraid that you are planning something in Blefuscu. He thinks you may be planning to destroy Lilliput,' the nobleman went on. 'Many
25 of the Emperor's men agree with the Admiral. They
have written down many things against you. They say
you are ungrateful. They say you are false to our Emperor and our country and many other things. They say
that your punishment should be death. Here is a copy of
30 their words.'

What I had done wrong

He brought out a long paper and all this was written
on it.

1. By an old law, no one is allowed to spit in the
palace gardens. The Man-Mountain spat there. He pretended to be putting out a fire.   5

2. The Man-Mountain brought back the ships from
Blefuscu to Lilliput. The King, our Emperor, asked him
to bring all the ships to Lilliput. Also, His Majesty asked
him to destroy all the enemies of Lilliput. The Man-
Mountain refused to do this. He pretended that the   10
people of Blefuscu had done nothing wrong.

3. When messengers came to Lilliput from Blefuscu
he greeted them kindly. He helped these servants of the
Emperor's enemies.

4. The Man-Mountain is planning to visit Blefuscu.   15
He will help the Emperor of Blefuscu who is the enemy
of our Emperor.

There were many other things on the paper but these
were the most important ones.

A plan to kill me

'His Majesty,' my friend told me, 'does not wish to   20
kill you. He wants you to leave Lilliput. But he does not
want you to help his enemy either.'

However, it seemed that the Admiral advised the Emperor to kill me at once. He wanted to put some poison*
in my food or shoot poisoned arrows at me.   25

Others were angry at this.

They said that the Emperor had given the Man-
Mountain his freedom. And the Man-Mountain had kept

---

*poison,   something which will cause sickness or death if
           eaten or drunk.

all his promises. It would be cruel to kill me after this.

Then one of the Emperor's advisers spoke out. He said that the citizens would be proud of their king if the Emperor was kind to the Man-Mountain. He advised the Emperor to take away his eyes and forgive him.

This adviser hated the Man-Mountain because his food cost such a lot of money. He said that the loss of eyes did not decrease strength. They would still be able to use the stranger's strength as they would be his advisers. They would tell him what to do and everybody would think they were very clever and kind.

But the rest of the Emperor's advisers were very angry. The Admiral had jumped up. This is what he said.

'Do you want to save the life of the Emperor's enemy? This man put out a fire by spitting. He can flood the palace if he wants to. He pulled the ships of Blefuscu to our harbour. He can also take them away at any time. He is dangerous. He should die.'

How the plan will be used

My friend told these things to me very sadly.

'His Majesty does not want to kill you but he wants to punish you,' he went on. 'Another officer said that we ought to give you less food. Then you would become smaller and smaller. At last you would be weak and you would die. Then we could cut your body into small pieces. People could bury these in faraway places. There would not be any smell and your bones could be kept to show to people now and in the future. I am afraid that everyone agreed to this plan except the Admiral. He wants you to be killed at once!'

My friend went on to tell me what the plan was.

'In three days' time,' he said, 'an official will come

to your home. He will tell you that the Emperor and all his officials are full of kindness. Twenty of the best doctors will be coming to take away your eyes. You must be helpful and lie down on the ground. Then they can shoot their arrows in your eyes. This is what the official 5 will tell you. He will not tell you that you will die from hunger later. He will repeat that the Emperor is fair and kind.'

My brave friend said that he must now leave my house secretly.   10

'Please think very carefully about my words,' he said as he was leaving. 'I hope you can plan something to help yourself this time.'

I thanked this true friend and put him gently outside.

I decide what to do

I remained alone. I felt sad and I was uncertain what   15 I ought to do.

Now the Emperor had a strange custom. At special meetings of his wise men he used to tell them that he was very kind. At once everyone knew that His Majesty was planning a cruel deed. I could not understand this.   20 I did not think it was kind to take away my sight. It was cruel, not kind or gentle at all.

At first I thought of asking the Emperor to forgive me. The facts were correct. I had done these things. Perhaps he would be kind but I knew that my enemies   25 would not be kind. They would not allow him to be kind either.

Then I thought that I would fight the whole of the Emperor's army. I could throw stones at the city. This would destroy the whole city easily. Then I remembered   30 something. All the people in Lilliput had been so kind to me. The Emperor too had been kind to me.

I go to Blefuscu

At last I decided to go to Blefuscu. I wrote to the Emperor's official and told him this. Later I went across to the harbour. I took one of the Emperor's ships and put all my clothes and goods in it. I jumped into the sea
5 and swam and walked to the port of Blefuscu. Two guides showed me the way to the capital city. I carried them with me until we were about two hundred yards from the city.

I sent the two guides to tell the King of Blefuscu's
10 officers about my arrival. I hoped they would arrange for me to see the Emperor.

After about one hour I got a reply. The Emperor with his family and his chief officers, was coming to see me. Soon afterwards, the Emperor and his family arrived.
15 They were not frightened of me at all. I lay on the ground to kiss the hand of the Emperor and the Queen. I wished to greet them very politely. They were very kind to me but I had great difficulty when I tried to find a house or somewhere to sleep.

Chapter 8

Three days after I had arrived in Blefuscu I went for a walk by the shore. In the sea, about half a mile away, I saw a strange thing. I pulled off my shoes and stockings and walked into the sea to take a look at it. It was a real European boat. But the bottom side was on top! 5 Perhaps it had been lost from a large ship during a storm.

Bringing the boat to the shore

I returned to the beach. I asked the Emperor to lend me twenty ships and three thousand sailors. He agreed and they sailed around the coast to meet me. I walked 10 back to the shore. The sea had carried the strange boat nearer. I went into the sea again. I swam behind the boat. Then with one hand I pushed and with the other hand I swam along. Soon the water only reached my shoulder so I could stand up in the water. The sailors 15 had made many ropes for me and I had twisted them together to make them stronger. Now the sailors threw these ropes to me but they fastened them to nine ships first of all. I fastened the ends of the ropes to the boat.

The ships pulled and I pushed the boat. We moved it 20 very near to the shore. I waited until the tide* was low. Then two thousand men with ropes and machines helped me to turn the boat over. I could not see much damage in the boat. Later and after much difficulty, I rowed into the harbour of Blefuscu. Thousands of peo- 25 ple came to watch for it was the biggest boat they had ever seen.

*tide,   rise and fall of the sea water caused by the moon each day.

A message from Lilliput

   I told the Emperor that it was very lucky that I had
found this boat. I begged him to allow me to mend it.
Then it could carry me back to my own country if I
received his permission to leave Blefuscu.

5   I did not receive any messages from Lilliput at this
time. Someone told me that the Emperor of Lilliput expected me to return there. He thought I did not know
about his cruel plans for me. Later, he sent a messenger
to the Emperor of Blefuscu.

'I must tell the Man-Mountain,' this messenger said, 'that if he will return to Lilliput, the Emperor will be very kind. He will only take away his eyes. My master expects you, the Emperor of Blefuscu, to send back this man. But first, his hands and feet must be tied 5 together.'

The Emperor thought about these words for a few days. He asked his officials to advise him. Then he sent this message to Lilliput.

'It is impossible for us to return this man to you. If 10 we tie his hands and feet we cannot move him. He has found a boat which is the right size for him. We should allow him to go to his own land as he costs both our countries so much to feed and to look after. This is the best plan.' 15

I prepare to leave

When I heard about these messages I decided to leave quickly. Five hundred workmen made two sails for my boat. They sewed thirteen pieces of their strongest cotton one on top of the other. I twisted together twenty
5   or thirty of their thickest ropes which made one good rope for me. On the sea-shore I found a large stone. This made a very good anchor.* The fat from three hundred sheep was rubbed on my boat. This was to stop any sea water from getting inside. I cut down some very large
10   trees. Then I cut some in smaller pieces to use with my sails. The other pieces I needed to row the boat. His Majesty's workmen helped to finish these for me.

It took about a month to get everything ready. I went to say good-bye to the Emperor and his family. All of
15   them came outside their beautiful home. I kissed the hand of the Emperor, his Queen and the princes. His Majesty gave me fifty purses. In each purse there were two hundred gold coins. He handed me a picture of himself which I put away carefully.
20   In the boat I carried the bodies of one hundred cattle and three hundred sheep. I also packed bread and wine as well as meat which had been cooked already. I wanted to show the cattle and sheep of Blefuscu to my own countrymen. So I took some live animals with me
25   and I took corn and dried grass to feed them. The Emperor made me promise that I would not take away any of his people. He looked in all my pockets before I was allowed to leave.

A ship finds me

I sailed away at 6 a.m. on 24 September 1701. After

*anchor,   iron hook placed on the bottom of the sea to keep
a ship from moving.

my boat had sailed about twelve miles I noticed a small
island. It was then about 6 p.m. on the same day. I
could not see any people so I put down my anchor. I
ate some food and then I went to sleep until the next
morning.   5

When I woke up I ate some more food. Then I pulled
up the anchor and I sailed to the north again. I did not
see anything all that day. On the third day I saw a sail
a long way away. I was afraid that no one would notice
me. But the ship came nearer and fired a gun. Then I 10
saw it showing a flag to me. I was so happy. My heart
was full of hope that, at last, I should see my country
and my dear family again.

Between five and six o'clock in the evening of 26
September I came near to the ship and I could see a 15
British flag. I put the cows and sheep in my pocket. I
packed up my food. When the ship came near to me I
was ready to get in it. I took as much as I could with me
on the sailing-ship.

I talk of my adventures

The name of the captain was John Biddell. He and 20
his fifty men had been to Japan. They were returning to
England through the South Seas. An old friend, called
Peter Williams, greeted me and he told Captain Biddell
all about me. This gentleman was most kind to me. He
asked many questions. Where had I come from? Where 25
was I going?

I told him about my adventures. He thought that I
was mad. He thought that the dangers in Lilliput and
Blefuscu had made me ill. I took the cattle and sheep
out of my pocket. I showed the captain the gold coins 30
from Blefuscu and also the picture of the Emperor. At
last Captain Biddell believed me. I gave him two purses

with two hundred gold coins in each of them. I promised to give him a cow and a sheep when we arrived in England.

It was 13 April 1702 when we reached England. All
5 my animals, except one sheep, travelled safely and as soon as possible, I put them in a field. The grass was thick and they began to eat at once. This made me happy as I had been worried about their health on our long journey.

I go on another journey
10 I showed these animals to many people in England. In this way, I made a lot of money. Later on, I sold them for six hundred pounds.

I stayed only two months with my wife and family. Then I wanted to see more foreign countries. I left
15 fifteen hundred pounds with my wife and I rented a good house for her. My wife and family would always have enough money as I now owned two houses. Johnny, my son, was doing well at school and my daughter, Betty, was at home with her mother. She
20 liked to sew and to look after things in the house.

I packed a lot of goods as well as money to take with me. I hoped to sell the goods at a high price. I travelled on the ship 'Adventure' which was sailing from Liverpool to Surat. When I said good-bye to my wife
25 and children we all cried sadly.

Part 2
A Voyage to Brobdingnag

Chapter 1

I left England on 20 June 1702, in the ship 'Adventure' with Captain John Nicholas. We reached the Cape of Good Hope safely. Then we discovered a crack in our ship. The sea water was coming in so we unloaded the cargo. We also decided to remain at the Cape of Good *5* Hope for the winter months.

Captain Nicholas became very ill with a fever so we did not return to the sea until March. About 19 April we passed Madagascar and the wind grew very strong. It blew us past the Molucca Islands and across the *10* Equator.*

Here the weather became calm and I was very glad about this after all the strong winds. But the captain said that another storm was coming. He was quite right. This time the winds blew us about one thousand five *15* hundred miles to the north-east. Nobody in the 'Adventure' knew where we were at all. However, our ship was strong and our health was good. We had plenty of food though the amount of fresh water was small. Captain Nicholas decided to steer towards the north. Then *20* we might reach the north coast of China and the Arctic seas.

*equator,   an imagined line round the earth at equal distances from the north and south poles.

Another adventure for me

We sailed on and on across the sea until 16 June 1703 when we saw land again. On 17 June we came close to the coast and our captain decided to search for fresh water.

5 We anchored outside a small harbour which was not deep enough for the 'Adventure' to sail in. Twelve men with jugs and bottles rowed to the shore in an open boat. I asked for permission to go with them. I always liked to see new countries and to make fresh discoveries.

10 When we stepped on the shore we could not see any rivers, streams or people. The sailors walked along the coast to find fresh water. I walked alone for about a mile on the other side. I could not see any grass or trees but only rocks. I became tired so I decided to return. I

15 saw that the sailors had already got in the boat. They were rowing back to the 'Adventure' as fast as they could. I wanted to shout to them. But just then I saw a very big man walking in the sea towards the boat. He walked quickly with big steps. There were many sharp

20 rocks in the sea so he had to stop. Soon the sailors were more than a mile away. The sight of this giant frightened me. I ran as fast as I could, away from the shore.

I meet many strange things

I climbed a steep hill so that I could see some of the countryside. The fields were full of crops but the grass

25 surprised me. It seemed to be twenty feet high.

I came to a main road. I discovered later that it was only a path across a field. I could not see very much for the corn was forty feet tall. It took me one hour to walk across this field. The bushes at the edge were a hundred

30 and twenty feet high and the trees were so tall that I could not see their tops.

There were some steps to climb before I could go to the next field. But each step was six feet high. I was trying to find a hole in the bushes when I saw someone coming. He was as tall as a church tower.* His footsteps were ten yards long. I was filled with fear and I ran to 5 hide myself in the corn. This person stood on the top step and shouted something. The noise of his shout went high in the air. At first I thought it was thunder. Then I saw seven monsters coming.

I try to run away
They carried great knives to cut the corn and each 10 knife was about the size of six of my knives. The first man gave an order. Immediately the other seven started to cut the corn near me. I crept away but I could not push through the thick corn easily. Then I had to stop. The corn was too thick. I could not move any more. 15 The men were very close now. I was very tired and I lay down. My thoughts were sad and I felt that I wanted to die. I thought of my wife and children. I remembered the words of my friends. They had advised me to stay at home but I had not listened to them. 20

I thought of Lilliput. The people there had thought I was the largest person in the world. Now I was the smallest in this place.

I was sure that these giants would eat me at once. One of them came nearer to me. I thought his knife 25 would cut me or that he would step on me. I screamed loudly for I was very frightened. The man looked all round. At last he saw me. He watched me carefully. Perhaps he thought I was a dangerous animal. Then he lifted me up and examined me carefully. I did not move. 30

*tower,   part of a building much taller than the rest of it,
          usually very strong.

I spoke very gently for I did not want to
make this man angry.

The farmer examines me
He looked at me with great interest.
My words seemed strange and wonderful
5   to him. Then I gave a cry of pain. He was
holding me very tightly and my sides were
hurting me. I turned my head down towards
them. He understood at once for he
put me gently inside his coat. Then
10 he ran to his master, the farmer.
This man looked at me even more
closely. He lifted up my coat. He blew my
hair away from my face. He asked his servant
if there were any more people in the fields
15 who looked like me. He put me on the
ground and I walked slowly back and forward
again. I did not try to run away.
The farmer and his workers now sat
down in a circle round me. I took off my hat
20 and bowed politely. I gave the farmer a purse.
He put it very close to his eyes. He turned it
round and round with the help of a pin. He
still did not know what it was. He then put
it back on the ground. I opened it and
25 gave him some gold coins. He wet the tip
of his little finger and lifted one of them up.
But he could not understand what they were.
He made a sign and I replaced the coins in
my purse.

The farmer takes me to his home

The farmer said many things to me. His words were clear but very loud and I could not understand a single word. I used different languages but it was useless.

Then he sent his workers back to the fields. He took
5   his handkerchief out of his pocket and spread it on the ground. He pointed to it and made signs to me. I understood his signs so I lay down on his handkerchief. He wrapped it round me and carried me to his house.

When he opened his handkerchief and showed me to
10 his wife, she screamed. However, she noticed that I seemed to understand her husband's signs. My behaviour pleased her and, after a little time, she began to like me.

It was now about midday. A servant brought in a dish about twenty four feet wide. It was filled with
15 meat. The farmer, his wife, their three children and their old grandmother began to eat. They put me on their table which was thirty feet high. I was so far from the ground that I was afraid I might fall over the edge.

The wife cut some meat and bread in small pieces.
20 She put them on a plate in front of me. I bowed very low and took out my own knife and fork. Everyone was pleased when I began to eat. A woman servant brought a small cup and filled it for me. It was very heavy and I lifted it with a lot of difficulty. I wished my hostess
25 'good health' but everyone laughed at my words. It was not water in the cup but it tasted very nice.

The farmer's youngest son

The master asked me to go to his plate. I walked along the table very carefully but there was a piece of bread which I did not notice in time. I fell flat on my
30 face. Luckily I was not hurt. I got up at once and spoke cheerfully to everyone.

The next minute the farmer's youngest son picked me up. He waved me in the air and I was frightened again. His father rescued me. He gave his son a heavy blow which would have knocked down a group of European horses. He ordered the boy to leave the table. He was *5* only ten years old and did not mean to be naughty. I went down on my knees and asked his father to forgive his son. The farmer understood my signs and the boy returned to the table. I kissed his hand and he now touched me gently. *10*

During dinner I heard a noise behind me like twelve machines. An animal had jumped on the knees of the farmer's wife. It was three times larger than a cow. She began to feed it and it was making this loud noise. It looked a very fierce animal to me. Then I saw that it *15* was a cat. The master made me stand about three yards away from this cat. It did not take any notice of me. I became a little braver and I walked closer to the cat's head. Soon three or four dogs came in. One was as big as four elephants but I was not so frightened of them. *20*

I become a baby's toy

Dinner was almost finished. Someone carried in a one-year-old boy. He thought I was a new toy and he screamed until his mother gave me to him. At once the little boy put my head in his mouth. I cried out loudly. The baby dropped me and I fell. I should have been *25* killed but the mother held out her dress. She caught me in this. The baby's nurse gave him a toy filled with large stones. He did not want this so she gave him some food. Then his loud cries stopped.

When dinner was ended the farmer went outside to *30* his workers. He told his wife to look after me very carefully.

I was very tired and I wanted to go to sleep. The farmer's wife put me on her own bed. Then she covered me with a clean white handkerchief which was as large as the sail of a big ship.

I kill a rat

5   I slept for about two hours. I dreamt that I was at home with my wife and children. This dream made me feel sad when I woke up.

The bedroom was between two and three hundred feet long and two hundred feet high. The bed I was
10 lying on was twenty yards wide and eight yards from the floor. I had been locked in the bedroom. Two rats suddenly crept towards me. They attacked me so I pulled out my sword. I hit one of them and the other ran away. The dead rat was about as big as a European
15 dog but its tail was almost two yards long. I walked up and down the bed for I was still feeling sad.

The wife came back soon after I had killed the rat. She saw all the blood and she picked me up quickly. I showed her that I was unhurt and this made her very
20 happy. A servant threw away the dead rat while I cleaned my sword. Then I put away my sword.

Chapter 2

Now the farmer had a daughter who was about nine
years old. She was very clever with her needle and she
helped to look after the baby also. This girl and her
mother changed a baby's bed into a bed for me. They
put it in a small drawer and this drawer was big enough   5
to make a complete bedroom for me.

She also made seven shirts for me. The cloth was the
smoothest in the country but it felt very rough to me.
She washed these shirts with her own hands. She became my teacher too. When I pointed to something she   10
told me its name. In a few days I was able to ask for
most things. Although she was only nine, she was eight
times taller than I was.

But she was very patient and kind. She looked after
me with the greatest care and remained at my side at all   15
times.

People must pay to see me

Soon more people heard about this strange animal
which the farmer had found in a field. They had heard
too that this animal was a tiny copy of a man.

A great friend of this farmer came to discover the   20
truth about me. I was placed on a table and I was told
to walk up and down. Then I had to show my sword
and make a polite bow to the farmer's guest.

'How do you do. I am very happy to meet you,' I said
to him.   25

This man put on his glasses as he was old and short-
sighted. I could not help laughing for his eyes looked
like the full moon when it was shining through two

windows. Other people started to laugh also and the old man became very angry.

He advised the farmer to take me to the market in the next town which was about twenty miles away. I could
5 not understand his words but I knew that they frightened me. Later the farmer's daughter told me about the plan. Her parents were going to show me to the townspeople. They would pay money to see and to touch me.

10 She began to cry for she thought these people might hurt me. She did not want ordinary men to pay to look at me. They might act roughly and rudely or even hurt me in some way. She told me something else. Her parents had promised to give me to her. Now they had
15 broken their promise and it was not the first promise that they had broken.

However, I was not so worried at this time. I thought that I might find a chance to get away from these people and this country.

A visit to the town
20 The next market day, we all rode to a nearby town on the farmer's horse. I was in a box with a few holes* in the sides to allow air to come in. The farmer's daughter had placed her own blanket in it for me to lie on. The journey lasted for half an hour but I was terribly
25 shaken all the time. The horse travelled about forty feet at every step and jumped high in the air too. I was thrown around like a ship in a great storm. My master stopped at an inn* in the town and talked to the owner for some time. The two of them paid a messenger to

*hole,   a place which has been dug or cut out.

*inn,   place where people may get food, drink, and may sleep there.

tell everybody in the town about a strange thing. This strange thing could be seen at the inn. It was almost human and it could do some amusing tricks.

I walked round the top of the table and bowed to them. Then I answered questions but I did not know *5* much of their language. I had to shout with my loudest voice or they would not have been able to hear me.

I wished them good luck as I lifted their smallest cup filled with wine.

I pulled out my sword and I waved it skilfully like a *10* proper swordman. Twelve times I repeated all my tricks until I could hardly stand up. My master did not allow anyone to touch me except his young daughter. He made all the visitors stand away from the table but one schoolboy threw a nut at my head. Luckily it just *15* missed me or it would have killed me.

We set out for the capital

Many people still wanted to see me so the farmer told everyone that he would return with me on the next market day.

He made a much better house for me now. This was *20* really necessary as I was so tired that I could hardly stand up or speak a word. It was three days before I felt strong again after that visit to the town.

Many gentlemen heard about me and came to see me at my master's house. I had very little rest even though *25* my master demanded the same price from a single family as he demanded from thirty people. However, I had a holiday every Wednesday as this was the rest day in this country.

I think that I had now been in this country for about *30* two months. My master decided to take me to the biggest cities in the kingdom. Then I could make more

money for him. He gathered together all the necessary
things for a long journey and he put his business in
order at home. On 17 August 1703 he said good-bye to
his wife and we set out for the capital which was about
three thousand miles away.   5

The journey to the capital

The farmer's daughter was riding behind her father. I
called her my little nurse as she looked after me so
well. She carried me in a box which was tied to her
waist. This box was as comfortable as she could make
it. There was soft cloth on all sides and she gave me her   10
doll's bed to sleep on. She found some clothing and
other things for me to use as well.

A boy servant rode behind with all the bags we
needed for our journey.

The farmer, my master, planned to show me in any   15
town we passed through. Usually we travelled about a
hundred and fifty miles each day because my little
friend complained that long rides tired her. She only
said this to help me.

She often lifted me out of my box to show me the   20
country and to give me some fresh air. We crossed several rivers: even the smallest river was bigger than the
River Thames in London. Our journey lasted for ten
weeks. People in eighteen towns as well as in many villages and small families had seen me during this time.   25

I am shown to many people

On 26 October we arrived at the capital. My master
rented some rooms in the most important street not far
from the palace. He rented another room between three
and four hundred feet wide. In it he placed a table sixty
feet wide with a three foot high wall on it. Therefore I   30
could not fall over the edge of the table.

Ten times each day I was shown to many people. I could now speak their language fairly well and could understand every word that the visitors said to me. I could also read a sentence or two as my little nurse car-
5   ried a religious book with her. From this book she taught me all the letters and explained all the words to me.

Chapter 3

With all my hard work in front of so many visitors my
health changed greatly. I grew very thin. My master became greedy and wanted to get even more money. He
saw that I looked very weak and he thought that I might
die soon. So he planned to make money quickly.   5

Just then a gentleman arrived from the palace. The
Queen and her ladies wished to see me immediately.
When she saw me the Queen was very pleased with my
behaviour. I fell on my knees and begged to kiss her
foot. She held out her little finger which I touched with 10
my lip. Then I was lifted on a table and she asked about
my country and my travels. I answered in a few words
as clearly as I could. The Queen asked me if I would like
to live at the palace. She asked if I would be happy
there. I bowed very low and answered that I belonged 15
to the farmer, but I should like to be useful to the
Queen. She asked my master whether he would sell me
for a good price.

I am sold to the Queen

He thought I would only live for one more month so
he was happy to lose me. He demanded one thousand 20
pieces of gold. These were given to him immediately.
I asked Her Majesty to allow my little nurse to remain
with me. She knew how to take care of me and she was
a good teacher too.

Her Majesty agreed to this. The farmer also agreed for 25
his daughter would now work in a palace. He was very
proud of her and the girl herself could not contain her
joy. My master pretended that he was sorry to leave me.

He told me that he had found a very good home for me.
He did not say anything about the money that the
Queen had given him. I bowed but I did not say a word
to him.

5   The Queen noticed this. She asked why I did not
speak to the farmer when he was leaving the palace. I
told Her Majesty about my hard life. I spoke about my
poor health and about the large amounts of money he
had got when he showed me to the public. He had only
10 let me go because I was ill. However, I knew that I
should have good care in the palace of the Queen. I told
her that I was feeling more cheerful. I said many beautiful yet true things to her but I spoke slowly and with
difficulty. I had only just learnt some of the correct
15 words on my way to the capital.

The King makes a mistake

The Queen was surprised by my wise words. She
picked me up and took me to see the King.

He thought I was a lizard* as he could not see me
clearly.

20 'My dear,' he said, 'I did not know that you were
fond of lizards.' He looked coldly at me.

The queen put me down on his desk and commanded
me to tell His Majesty all about myself. I did this in a
very few words.

25 My little friend had followed the Queen as she worried about me all the time. She now spoke up and
agreed with my story. Everything that had happened
since I had arrived at her father's house was true.

The King was a very clever man, as clever as anyone
30 in his kingdom. Yet at first he thought that I was a toy.
He was most surprised to hear my voice but he did not

*lizard,   small long-tailed cold-blooded animal.

believe my story completely. He thought the farmer and his daughter had taught me lies so that they could get more money when they sold me. Therefore he asked me many questions. He received true answers. Next, three of the King's wisest men examined me. They decided *5* that I was a freak.* The smallest man they knew was at least thirty feet tall. These men said I was very unusual but I replied that they were mistaken. In my own country there were millions of people exactly like me.

The King acts wisely

They then said that the farmer had taught me this. *10* They believed that I repeated whatever he had told me.

The King was much cleverer than these three men. He sent for the farmer and for his daughter. He saw them separately and asked many questions. Then he asked me to repeat my story. My replies were satisfac- *15* tory. He felt that I was telling the truth. He asked the Queen to take the greatest care of me. He too wanted the farmer's daughter to look after me.

So the Queen gave her a room at the palace with two servants for herself. She was given a teacher too and her *20* only duty was to take care of me.

My new house and clothes

Next, the Queen ordered her furniture-maker to make a special wooden bedroom for me. It was made out of a box, sixteen feet square and twelve feet high. It had windows, a door and two cupboards. The top of this *25* box could be lifted out. Every day when my nurse tidied my bed she just took off this roof. She hung the blanket outside and then at night she returned the complete bed to me.

**freak,*   a most unusual person, animal, etc.

A clever workman made two chairs, two tables and a smaller cupboard. The walls, the floor and ceiling of the box were covered with several pieces of cloth. These were sewn together to protect me from any accident.
5   Another workman made a key for the door. It was the smallest he had ever made. I kept this key in my own pocket and locked my door to stop rats from coming in.

The Queen ordered some clothes for me. They were
10   made from their thinnest silk but they were as heavy as blankets to me. Now my clothes looked the same as the other people's clothes.

I have dinner with the Queen
The Queen liked me so much that she could not have dinner without me. She gave me a chair and a table on
15   her own table next to her elbow. My nurse stood on a stool nearby to help me. I was given my own silver dishes and plates and my nurse kept them in a silver box. She washed these dishes herself. Only the two princesses aged sixteen and thirteen, had dinner with the
20   Queen.

Her Majesty used to place a piece of meat on my plate. She laughed when I cut small pieces off. She herself ate in one small mouthful as much as twelve English farmers could eat at one meal. I thought this was very
25   unpleasant. Sometimes she put the wing of a bird nine times larger than a large chicken in her mouth. She broke the bones with her teeth and then swallowed everything. She drank about fifty-two gallons* at once out of a gold cup. In her mouth she often put a piece of

*gallon,   a fixed amount of something like water, oil, wine,
            etc.

bread as big as two of our largest loaves. Her knives, forks and spoons were twice as long as tools for cutting corn. It was a terrible sight to see ten or twelve of these knives when someone lifted them up together. It frightened me very much. 5

The King asks many questions

Every Wednesday, which was the rest day, the King and Queen with all their children had dinner together. I was now a great favourite with the King. At these times my little table and chair were put on his left hand side. The King used to ask me about the laws, govern- 10 ment, religion and manners of Europe. I told him all that I knew. He spoke very wisely about all these things. Perhaps I spoke too proudly about my own country for suddenly he began to laugh.

'You are a tiny insect,' he said, 'and yet you seem to 15 copy the ways of my country. You seem to have towns and cities. Your people have the same behaviour as mine.'

He went on talking about my country in an annoying way. My great and strong country seemed so small and 20 unimportant to him. At first the King's words made me angry. Then I thought about them carefully. I remembered how strange everything had appeared to me at first in the King's country. Now I was used to the size of everything. Perhaps the sight of ordinary people 25 might make me laugh too.

The smallest men in the country

Sometimes the Queen placed me on her hand. Then we looked in her mirror together. It was so funny to compare the size of the Queen with my size. I began to

think that I had become much smaller than my proper size.

The smallest man in the country before I arrived was a dwarf.* He was about thirty feet tall and he belonged to the Queen too. He made me very angry. He pre- *5* tended that he was so big and that I was so small. He hurt me with his unkind words about my height. In return I called him 'my brother'. One day, during dinner, this dwarf was very angry with me because of my words to him. He picked me up round my waist. He dropped *10* me into a large silver bowl of cream. I fell completely in this cream. My nurse was at the other end of the room. The Queen was too frightened to help me. I was in great difficulty but luckily, I was a good swimmer. I managed to swim until my nurse ran to help me. She pulled me *15* out but I had swallowed about a quart of cream.

I went to bed at once. However, I was unhurt although my clothes were completely spoiled. The dwarf was given a beating and the Queen commanded him to drink all the cream in the bowl. Soon afterwards, the *20* Queen gave the dwarf to a friend and I did not see him again.

*dwarf,   a person, plant or animal that is much smaller than usual.

Chapter 4

The King quite often travelled to the far ends of his kingdom. I now knew that it was called Brobdingnag. It was more than six thousand miles in length and three to five thousand feet wide. The Queen also went with him
5 but she did not travel all the way. I went with her and I noticed many things.

I began to think that the maps in Europe were not correct. They showed only an ocean between Japan and California in America. I now believed that Brobdingnag
10 should be joined to the north-west of America. Brobdingnag is a peninsula.* It ends with a line of mountains which are thirty miles high. These throw out gases, smoke and fire. There is not a single sea-port in the country. The sea on all three sides is very stormy and
15 there are many pointed rocks where the rivers flow into the seas. Therefore the people here never buy or sell goods to the rest of the world.

Large ships sail on the rivers which are full of good fish. The sea-fish are the same size as those in Europe so
20 they do not catch them. They are too small for them to eat.

My new travel-box
The Queen ordered her workmen to build a travel-box for me so that I could go with her when she went to the country. It was smaller than my house-box, and was
25 about twelve feet square and ten feet high. My nurse was able to hold this on her knees when we travelled around. This little house had windows in three of the

*peninsula,   a piece of land which has water on three sides.

walls. These were covered with thick wire to protect
them. On the fourth wall on the outside of the box,
there were two strong pieces of curved metal. A leather
belt could be put through these and the belt was then
fastened round a servant's waist. This meant that I could   5
ride on horseback with a servant.

I could see the country very well through the three
windows. I had a table and two chairs which were fastened to the floor. I also had a bed which was made
from strong cloth. This bed was hung down from the   10
ceiling so now I need not be thrown about when we
were travelling.

All things are large to me

One day I went to see the chief temple in the land.
It disappointed me for it was not as tall as I had expected. But it was very beautiful and very strong. The   15
stone walls were a hundred feet thick. Figures of gods
and kings were placed in spaces all over the walls. A
finger had fallen off one of the figures. It was four feet
and one inch in length. My nurse wrapped it in her
handkerchief and took it home in her pocket.   20

The King's kitchen was another large building. The
oven* in which the King's food was cooked, was as wide
as the curved roof of the largest church in London. I do
not think you will believe me if I tell you the exact size
of the pots, the pans or the pieces of meat there. You   25
will think that I am imagining all this. But if the King
and people of Brobdingnag ever read this, they will feel
annoyed. They will say that I have not told the truth. I
have not described things as big as they truly are!

His Majesty owned about six hundred horses which   30
were all fifty to sixty feet tall. When he made any spe-

*oven,   a box-like space which is heated and used to cook food.

cial visits to any place, he had a guard of five hundred horses. This was a wonderful sight but the King's army was an even better sight.

Chapter 5

I was quite happy in Brobdingnag but my small height
led to several accidents. My nurse often carried me to
the palace gardens where I walked around. One day before the dwarf left the Queen, I made a silly joke about
dwarf apple trees. This is the correct name for these   5
trees in my own country but it annoyed him. So when
I was walking under one of these dwarf apple trees he
shook it over my head. Twelve apples as large as water-
cans fell down. I was knocked flat on my face. The
dwarf was not punished this time because I had made   10
him angry first.

Another day I was sitting on the grass in the garden.
My nurse was walking around with her teacher. Suddenly there was a storm of hailstones* which struck me to
the ground. I crept into some shelter near a row of   15
plants. I could not go outside again for ten days because
I had so many painful lumps on my body.

Another accident

A more dangerous accident happened to me in the
same garden. My nurse had left my travel-box at home
and she put me in a safe place. Then she went to an-   20
other part of the garden to talk to her teacher. While she
was away the gardener's dog got in the garden when nobody was looking. It smelled me and came running up.
Then it took me in its mouth and ran straight to its
master. Luckily the dog had been taught how to carry   25
things carefully and I was not hurt. My clothes were not
even torn. The poor gardener, who knew me well, was in

*hailstone,   ball of ice that falls like rain.

a terrible fright. He picked me up gently and asked if I was hurt. I was so surprised and so breathless that I could not speak. After a few minutes I felt better so the gardener carried me back. By this time my nurse had
5 returned to the place where she had left me. She was very worried because she could neither see nor hear me. When the gardener appeared she scolded him because of his dog. Nobody in the palace heard about this accident for the girl was afraid of the Queen's anger. I did not
10 want to tell anybody about it either.

Adventures with birds

My nurse now decided to keep me in her sight all the time. I liked to be alone sometimes so I had not told her about some of my early adventures. Once a big bird tried to carry me away. I pulled out my sword and then
15 ran under some bushes. On another day I fell into a hole which an animal had dug. I remember that I had to make up an excuse because my clothes were spoiled. Once I fell over the shell of a snail* and cut my leg.

The smaller birds in the garden were not afraid of me.
20 They used to hop about my feet as they looked for food. They picked food out of my hand. But when I tried to catch one of them it bit my fingers. Then it hopped back to the same place again. One day I threw a thick stick at a bird and I knocked it down. I ran to my
25 nurse, holding the bird round the neck with both my hands. The bird was not badly hurt by my stick and it began to beat me with its wings. I held it away from my body but it gave me so many blows that I had to let it go.

*snail,   small animal that carries a shell on its back.

A boat is made for me

I often talked about sea-voyages so the Queen asked if I could row a boat. She thought that rowing would be good for my health. I said that I could both row and sail a boat. However, the smallest rowing-boat in Brobdingnag was bigger than an English warship. Then Her *5* Majesty asked me to make a plan of a boat. Then her workman could make one and she promised to find a place where I could row and sail. Her workman was very skilful and in ten days he finished one for me. It was large enough to hold eight ordinary people. When the *10* Queen saw it, she was very pleased. At once she took it to the King who ordered it to be put in a bowl of water. But this was too small and I could not use the oars.* The Queen thought of another plan. Her workmen now made a wooden box, three hundred feet long, fifty feet *15* wide and eight feet deep. This was placed in an outer room of the palace, on the floor. At the bottom there was a tap so that dirty water could flow away. It took two servants half an hour to fill this box with water.

I fight with a frog

I often rowed for enjoyment now and the Queen and *20* her ladies liked to watch. They were very pleased with my skill. Sometimes I used the sails. Then I only had to steer for the ladies blew me along with their fans. When they were tired of doing this, the younger servants blew me along with their own breath. Afterwards, my little *25* nurse always carried my boat back to her cupboard. There she hung it on a nail to dry.

I was almost killed one day when I was getting ready for a sail. My nurse's teacher lifted me up to place me in the boat. I slipped out of her hand. It was forty feet *30*

*oars,   a stick with a flat end, used to row a boat.

to the ground. By a lucky chance a pin in her dress caught my shirt and trousers. I was hanging in the air until someone lifted me down.

5 Another time a servant was filling my pond with fresh water. He was careless and allowed a frog to slide into the water. The frog hid at the bottom of the pool until I was sailing in my boat. Then it climbed up and sat on one edge. It almost sank the boat as it was such a heavy frog. Then it hopped forward and back again over my 10 head. Each time it left some soft mud on my face and clothes. It seemed a very ugly frog to me. I hit it many times with my oar and at last I made it jump out of my boat.

A monkey causes trouble

But it was a monkey that caused the greatest danger.
15 My nurse had locked me up in her room while she did something else. It was very warm weather so the window was open. The windows and door in my box were open too. I was sitting at my table when I heard something jump through the window in the next room.

20 It skipped from one side to the other: I was quite frightened. I looked out but did not move from my chair. A care-free monkey was jumping up and down. Then it noticed my box. It took a short quick look through every window and the door. Quickly I moved
25 to the back of the room. I was too frightened to think calmly so I did not hide under the bed. This was a big mistake. The monkey talked and laughed to itself outside my room. Then it saw me. It stretched out its arm to hold me. I moved round from corner to corner. But
30 the monkey played with me as a cat plays with a mouse. At last it took hold of my coat and it dragged me out.

It lifted me up and held me just like a baby. I tried hard to move but the monkey squeezed me tightly. It was wiser to keep still. The monkey touched my face gently. It must have thought I was a young one of its own kind. Then it heard a noise outside my nurse's room. Somebody was opening the door.

I am trapped on the roof

The monkey leaped up to the window through which it had climbed in. It still held me as it walked along the gutters until it reached the roof of the next building. I heard my nurse screaming as the monkey carried me outside. She was almost mad with fear. At once that part of the palace was filled with noise and excitement. The servants ran for ladders. Hundreds of people watched as the monkey sat on the top edge of the roof.

It was still holding me like a baby in one arm. With the other arm the monkey was pushing food in my mouth. It hit me gently on the back when I would not eat. Many people could not help laughing at this sight. I could not blame them as it looked funny to everyone except myself.

Some of the people began to throw stones to bring the monkey down. But this was soon stopped for it was dangerous to me. Several men climbed up the ladders. The monkey was almost caught. It could not run quickly if it carried me. So it dropped me on the top of the roof and hurried away. I was now about five hundred feet from the ground. Every minute I thought I might fall or the wind might blow me over. Everything seemed to be turning round and round in front of me when a young servant reached me. He put me in the pocket of his trousers and then he carried me down the ladder.

My adventure amuses the King

I could not breathe properly because the monkey had pushed so much nasty-tasting food down my throat. My little friend picked it all out with a needle. This helped me very much. But I was so weak and sore from the
5 monkey's squeezes that I had to remain in bed for two weeks. The King, the Queen and all their ladies and gentlemen asked about my health every day. Her Majesty visited me several times.

The monkey was killed later and no more monkeys
10 were allowed to come near the palace.

I went to see the King when I felt better to thank him for his kindness to me. He laughed about my adventure. He asked me about my thoughts when the monkey was holding me on the roof. He wanted to know if I liked
15 the food it had given to me. He asked if I liked the way in which the food had been pushed in my mouth. He thought that all the fresh air I had received on the roof would make me feel hungry. Then he asked what I would have done if a monkey had attacked me in my
20 own country.

I try to explain

I told His Majesty that we did not have many monkeys in Europe. People sometimes brought them from other lands but then the monkeys were very small. I could defend myself from twelve like this at a time, if
25 they attacked me. But the monkey which had carried me away was as large as an elephant. I think that if I had remembered to use my sword I could have hurt it a little. I could have made it run away. But I was too frightened to pull out my sword. I told all this to the
30 King so that he would not call me a coward.

However, the King and all his gentlemen laughed

loudly. They thought that I was boasting again. It was difficult to make them understand for I was so different from them. Yet I have seen the same sort of behaviour now that I have returned to England. There are some boastful people who say that they are as clever and as 5 wise as the greatest in the land.

I fall into a muddy pool

Every day something seemed to happen to me. My nurse loved me very much. Yet she always told the Queen whenever I did anything foolish. Then the Queen would laugh at me. 15

One day my nurse, her teacher and I went for a drive in the fresh air. They stopped near a path in a field and put my travel-box down. I went out of this to take a walk. There was a muddy pool of water in the path. I tried to jump over it and I landed in the middle with 20 water up to my knees. I walked through the pool with difficulty.

One of the menservants wiped my clothes with his handkerchief. I was very muddy and dirty and had to go in my travel-box at once. 25

The Queen was told about this. The servant told many people too so that there was much laughter about me for many days.

Chapter 6

I always believed that one day I should be free again. It was impossible to say how this might happen. I could not think of a plan that might be successful. The ship in which I had arrived was the first to be seen near
5 Brobdingnag. The King now gave orders about any ship that might be seen in the future. He wanted it to be pulled to the shore. Then the ship with all its sailors and passengers must be brought to the capital in a goods lorry.

I wish to be free
10   The King wished me to marry someone of my own size and to have a family. From the passengers he would be able to find a wife for me. I thought that death would be better than leaving children to live in cages. I was treated with great kindness. I was the favourite of
15 a great King and Queen and all their friends. But my children might be sold to people in the kingdom. They might have masters like the farmer who only wanted to make money.
    This was not the proper way to live. I never forgot
20 those I had left behind in Europe. Now I wanted to talk to people who were equal to me. I wished to walk about freely, without fear. In this country someone might step on me and kill me at any moment. I was always afraid from day to day.
25   However, I became free sooner than I had expected.

A journey to the coast
    At the beginning of my third year the King and

Queen visited the south of Brobdingnag. I was carried
with them in my travel-box which was now very comfortable. A special bed was hung by silk ropes from the
four corners in the ceiling. I did not swing about so
much when a servant carried my box on horseback. I   5
could sleep in this bed while we travelled along the
roads. In the ceiling a wood-worker made a hole which
was a foot square. This gave me fresh air when I was
asleep. I could pull a board over this hole to close it.

The King decided to stay for a few days at a place   10
eighteen English miles from the sea shore. My nurse and
I were very tired and I had caught a cold. My nurse was
so ill that she had to stay in her room but I wanted to
see the ocean. I felt sure that one day I would escape
over the sea. I pretended to be very unwell. I told my   15
nurse that I needed fresh sea air. My nurse and friend
did not want me to go without her. But at last she gave
permission to a young man who had taken me out before. I liked him very much. My nurse begged him to
take great care of me. She burst into tears when I left   20
her. She seemed almost afraid to let me go out.

An eagle carries me away

This young man carried me in my box for about half
an hour. We reached the seashore and I asked him to put
me down on the rocks. I opened a window and looked
sadly at the sea. I did not feel well so I decided to have   25
a short rest in my swinging bed.

The young man shut the window for me as it was
quite cold. I soon went to sleep. I think the servant
went to look for birds' eggs among the rocks. He
thought that there was no danger to me anywhere there.   30

I woke up suddenly. Something was pulling the ring
on top of my box. I felt that my box was being raised

high in the air. Then we were going forward at a great
speed. I almost fell out of bed when my travel-box was
lifted up so roughly. Then the movement grew much
smoother.

5   I called out several times as loudly as possible. But it
was useless. I looked through my windows. I could see
only the sky and clouds. I heard a noise like the sound
of wings over my head. I began to understand what had
happened. An eagle—for it must be a very big bird—had

10   picked up the ring on my box in its beak.* It planned to
break open the box on a rock. The bird thought that my
box was a shell with an animal inside it. Then it would
eat me.

I fall into the sea

       After a time the noise from the wings of birds grew

15   louder. My box was thrown up and down like a leaf on
a windy day. Then I felt I was falling straight down for
about a minute. The box fell so quickly that I almost
lost my breath. There was a terrible splash. I was in
darkness for another minute. Then my box began to rise

20   and I could see light from the top of my windows. I
now saw that I had fallen in the sea. About five feet of
the box was under the water. Luckily for me the plates
of iron at the bottom of the box had protected it. They
also kept the box standing straight up.

25   Now the door did not open like other doors. Instead
it moved up and down so very little water came in. I got
out of bed with much difficulty but first I pushed back
the board in the roof. I could hardly breathe until I had
done this.

30   I wished that I could go back to my dear friend and
nurse again. I was very sorry for myself but I was also

       *beak,   the hard part of a bird's mouth.

sorry for her. She would be sad because she had lost me
and the Queen would be very angry with her. There
would not be any work for her at the palace so her
father would be angry with her too.

Many fears and difficulties

At this time I had to face many difficulties. I thought   5
a high wave might break my box. A strong wind might
blow me over. I would die immediately if the glass in
the windows was broken. I saw that a little water was
coming in through several cracks. They were not large
cracks so I tried to close them up. I was not able to lift   10
off the roof of my box so I could not sit on top of it. If
the danger from the wind and sea did not kill me, I was
sure that I would die from hunger and cold. I sat thinking like this for four hours. I thought that each minute
was to be my last one before I died.   15

Now on the side of my box which had no window in
it, there were two pieces of metal. The servant used to
put his belt through them when we travelled on horseback. I thought I heard a noise coming from that side of
the box. I thought my box was being pulled over the   20
sea. It did not seem to be just moving without direction.
The waves sometimes rose to the top of the windows
and left me in the dark. Yet I started to hope that help
was coming. But I was unable to imagine who could
help me.   25

I hope to be saved

I unscrewed one of the chairs and placed it under the
air-hole. Then I climbed on the chair. I put my mouth
as near to the hole as I could. I shouted for help in every
language that I understood.

Next I tied my handkerchief to a stick and I pushed   30

it through the air-hole. I waved it several times in the
air. I hoped that the sailors in any nearby ship would
see it. I wanted them to know that there was someone
alive inside the box.

5   But nothing happened. Yet I knew that I was moving
along. I knew that something was pulling me. After
about an hour the windowless side of my box hit something hard. I was afraid that it was a rock. The box
seemed to be jumping up and down. Then I heard a
10   noise over my head. It sounded like a rope which was
being tied to the ring on the roof.

Now the box was being pulled up. I pushed out my
stick and handkerchief. I shouted for help until my
throat was sore. Then I heard a great shout which was
15   repeated three times. I was filled with joy. I heard the
sound of feet over my head. Then somebody called
through the hole in English.

'Is there anybody below? Answer if there is!'

I am thought to be mad

I at once said that I was an English doctor and I had
20   been in great danger. I begged the speaker to get me out
of my prison. He told me that I was safe now. My box
had been fastened to his ship and a sailor was coming to
saw a larger hole. Then I could be pulled out. I replied
that this would take too long. It would be easier for a
25   sailor to put his finger through the ring itself. Then he
could lift the whole box out of the sea and carry it to
the ship's captain.

The sailors thought that I was speaking wildly. Some
thought I was mad while others laughed at me. I did not
30   understand that I was among people of my own height
and strength.

Soon a hole about four feet square was made in the

roof. A man held a small ladder for me and I climbed up. I was taken carefully onto the ship but I was feeling very weak.

Ail the sailors were very surprised and asked me many questions. I did not feel well enough to reply. I was sur- *5* prised to see how small everybody was. I was comparing them with the people I had left so recently.

My travel-box sinks

The captain of the ship, Mr. Thomas Wilcocks, noticed my weak condition. He took me to his room and gave me a hot drink to comfort me. He offered me his *10* own bed and advised me to take a rest. I needed a good sleep. Before I went to sleep though, I told Mr. Wilcocks about my travel-box. There was some good furniture in it, a bed, two chairs, a table and a cupboard with shelves and drawers. There was silk and cotton on all the *15* walls. Everything was too good to be lost.

I asked the captain to let one of his sailors bring the box to this room. Then I would show him all my goods. The captain too thought that I was speaking wildly. However, he promised to give the necessary orders as I *20* think he wanted to calm me.

He went outside and sent some men down to my travel-box. These men pulled down the silk and cotton and brought out the rest of my goods. The chairs, cupboard and bed were badly damaged by these men. They *25* tore them roughly out of the floor to which they had been fastened. Next they pulled out some of the wooden boards to use on the ship. When they had got all they wanted they let the box drop in the sea. It sank at once as there were so many holes in it. I was glad that *30* I did not see all this. I did not want to be reminded of the past years. I only wanted to forget them.

How the captain found me

I slept for several hours. I had many unpleasant dreams about Brobdingnag and my dangerous adventures. Hoever, I felt much better when I woke up.

It was now about eight o'clock and the captain ordered some supper. It was a long time since I had eaten anything. Mr. Wilcocks spoke kindly to me and advised me not to look round so wildly nor to talk foolishly. He asked me to tell him about my travels. He also wanted to know why I was floating on the sea in my wooden box.

At first he had thought my box was a sail. When he had discovered his mistake he sent a boat with several sailors to take a look. His men returned and they were very frightened. They said they had seen a swimming house! The captain said he had laughed at them. Then he decided to look at the 'swimming house' himself, taking a strong rope with him.

He rowed round me several times and noticed the windows with wire over them. When he noticed the two iron hooks he ordered his men to row to that side. Next he fastened his rope through the hooks. Then he told his men to pull the box towards his ship.

When they had returned to the ship another rope was fastened through the ring on the top of the box. All his sailors pulled this rope but they could only lift the box about three feet. The captain said they saw my handkerchief and stick. They knew then that someone must be shut inside.

The captain is troubled

I asked Mr. Wilcocks whether he or his men had seen any big birds in the sky about this time. One sailor said he had noticed three eagles flying towards the north. He did not think that they were any bigger than usual. No-one guessed the reason for my question.

    ' I next asked how far we were from the land. At least three hundred miles was the answer. I was sure this must
5 be a mistake. I could not have travelled so far from Brobdingnag in a few hours. Mr. Wilcocks thought my brain was still unsettled. He advised me to go to bed and to rest again. I told him that I was quite well and that there was nothing wrong with my brain. He then spoke
10 to me seriously.

    He asked if I had done any bad deeds. He had wondered to himself whether I was being punished. Sometimes wicked men were punished in this way. They were sent across the ocean in a boat without food.

15 His said that he did not like carrying a bad man on his ship. Yet he was sorry for me and he said he would set me safely on shore at the first harbour that we came to. He could not help feeling that something was wrong when I made several silly speeches to his sailors. He
20 thought I had behaved strangely during supper and I had talked foolishly about my travel-box.

I tell the truth

    I begged him to hear my story. I told him about everything, from the last time I left England to the minute he had discovered me. Truth always succeeds. This
25 honest man soon felt certain that I was telling the truth. I asked him to bring my cupboard to his room. I could show things to him from the country I had just left.

    The cupboard was brought to me and I opened it with a key from my pocket.

30 I showed him my strange collection. There was a comb I had made out of hair from the King's chin. Another comb had a back which I had made from part

of the thumb-nail of the Queen. There were pins and needles from twelve to eighteen inches long; some of the Queen's hair; even four stings* as large as nails from an insect. There was a gold ring which the Queen used to wear on her little finger. One day she had thrown it over my head like a collar. I asked the captain to accept this ring in return for his kindness to me. He refused to do this.

Last of all I showed him my trousers which were made from the skin of a mouse.

The captain accepts a present

Mr. Wilcocks would not accept anything from me except the tooth of a servant. He examined it carefully and wanted to keep it. I thought this was a small present to give him but he thanked me over and over again for it. This tooth had been pulled out by mistake as it was really a good one. It was about a foot long and four inches wide and after it was cleaned I had kept it in my cupboard.

The captain thought my story was satisfactory. When we returned to England he hoped that I would write a book about my adventures. I thought that there were too many travel-books already and I did not think I had anything new to write about. I believed that many writers did not always tell the truth. However, I thanked him for his interest. I promised to think about it.

One thing puzzled Mr. Wilcocks. He said that I spoke very loudly and he thought the King and Queen of Brobdingnag must have been deaf. I told him that I had listened to these loud voices for over two years. He and his men seemed to me to be whispering. Yet I could

*sting, sharp pointed part of an insect or plant. Can cause
          poisoning or pain.

hear them very well. In that other country when I spoke
to anyone it seemed like shouting to the top of a church
tower.

I find everything small

5   Also at first, the sailors on this ship seemed to be the
smallest creatures I had ever seen. I said that in Brobdingnag I had stopped looking in mirrors. They made
me feel so small and unimportant.

The captain noticed that I looked surprised when we
were eating. I appeared to be laughing at everything.
10 This was true. To me, the dishes looked like coins. The
meat was hardly a mouthful and the cups were like nut-
shells. All the captain's goods looked tiny for I had
become used to large sizes in everything. I forgot that
I was the same size as the captain. I only remembered
15 the strange country of Brobdingnag.

The captain thought I was joking. He wished he had
seen my travel-box in the eagle's beak. He also wished
he had seen the box when it fell in the sea. He would
have paid a lot of money to see these wonderful sights.

I return to England

20 The ship sailed on its way and was blown far away
to the south. We passed the Cape of Good Hope twice
on our way back to Europe as we were blown back and
then forward again. The captain visited a few towns
where he bought food and water. The voyage was suc-
25 cessful for him and he earned much money and many
goods.

I did not leave the ship until we arrived in England on
3 June 1706. This was about nine months after I left
Brobdingnag. I offered to leave my goods to pay for my
30 fare. But the captain would not take anything at all. We

said good-bye in a friendly manner and I made him promise to visit me at my house.

I needed a horse and a guide so I borrowed a little money from him to pay for them.

As I travelled along the roads I thought I was in Lilli- *5* put again. The houses, trees, people and cattle looked so small. I was afraid of stepping heavily on every traveller I met. I often asked them to stand out of my way.

Home at last

I had to ask someone where my house was. When a servant opened the door I bent down to go in. I was *10* afraid of hitting my head. My wife ran to kiss me. I bent down lower than her knees as I thought she could not reach my mouth. My daughter knelt before me but I could not see her until she stood up. My head and eyes were used to looking about sixty feet up in the air. I put *15* my arm round my daughter's waist. I looked down at the servants and one or two friends and I felt like a giant.

I told my wife that she had been too careful with money. She and my daughter looked so small to me that *20* I did not think she had been buying enough food. I behaved so strangely that they feared I was mad. Mr. Wilcocks had thought this when he first saw me too. It shows that habits are very strong. They can be difficult to change. *25*

In a little time, my family and friends and I understood what had happened. My wife said that I should not go to sea again. But I could not order my future life myself.

My readers may know more about my life at a later *30* time. Now I have come to the end of my story about two of my voyages.

Questions

Part 1

9. What would happen if a flame touched the gun-powder?

10. Give the names of the things that were not returned to Gulliver.

Chapter 3

1. What things about Gulliver pleased the Emperor?

2. Who would not agree to set Gulliver free?

3. What did Gulliver do while he was making some promises?

4. Was he allowed to lie on the grass?

5. If the Emperor wanted to send a message very quickly, who would send it for him?

6. Where did the enemies of Lilliput live?

7. Where were the stones going after Gulliver had lifted them?

8. How much food was Gulliver allowed?

9. Who had decided how much food he should be given?

10. Was Gulliver allowed to lift up any citizens?

Chapter 4

1. What was the name of the capital of Lilliput?

2. How high was the wall round the city?

3. Why didn't Gulliver wear his coat when he went out for a walk?

4. Where was the Emperor's palace?

5. Why couldn't Gulliver see the inside buildings?

6. What did he make after he cut down some trees?

7. Why did he make these articles?

8. Who did he see inside the palace?

9. Who went to visit Gulliver in the temple?

10. What was the Emperor most afraid of in Blefuscu?

Chapter 5   1. How far was Blefuscu from Lilliput?
2. Where were the ships of Blefuscu?
3. What did Gulliver fasten to the enemy ships?
4. Why didn't these ships move when he pulled so hard?
5. What did Gulliver use to protect his eyes?
6. What did the people of Blefuscu do when they understood what was happening?
7. What reward did the Emperor give to Gulliver for his work?
8. Why did the Emperor become very angry with Gulliver?
9. Why wasn't the Queen happy when Gulliver put out the fire at the palace?
10. How big were the buckets of water the people used?

Chapter 6   1. What was the punishment for cheating in Lilliput?
2. Why did the statue of Justice have six eyes?
3. Which is more important in Lilliput — ability or behaviour?
4. Why were children taken away from their parents? Give 2 reasons.
5. How many times could parents visit their children?
6. How long did children remain at school?
7. What did the tailors do to make their cloth thicker?
8. Why did Gulliver's clothes look so unusual?
9. How many cooks prepared food for him?
10. Which country did Gulliver wish to visit?

Chapter 7   1. How did Gulliver discover that there was a secret plan against him?

2. What did the Emperor think that Gulliver would do in Blefuscu?
3. What was the name given to Gulliver in Lilliput?
4. Who advised the Emperor to kill Gulliver at once?
5. How did he think Gulliver ought to be killed?
6. What would happen if Gulliver had been given less and less food?
7. Why did Gulliver decide not to destroy the city?
8. What plan was agreed to by everyone?
9. How did Gulliver get to Blefuscu?
10. How did he find the way to the main city?

Chapter 8   1. What did Gulliver find in the sea?
2. How did he make stronger ropes for himself?
3. Why did Gulliver wish to mend the boat?
4. Why was it impossible for the Emperor of Blefuscu to send Gulliver back to Lilliput?
5. What did Gulliver use for an anchor?
6. Why was sheep-fat rubbed on Gulliver's boat?
7. What did the Emperor give to Gulliver as a present?
8. Why did Gulliver take some live animals as well as dead ones with him?
9. For how many days did Gulliver sail before he was rescued?
10. How long did he remain in England this time?

Part 2

Chapter 1
1. Why did Gulliver's ship unload its cargo?
2. Why did Gulliver go to the shore with the crew who were looking for water?
3. Why did the sailors row to the ship without him?
4. What did Gulliver think the giant's shout was?
5. What did Gulliver give to the farmer?
6. How did the farmer carry Gulliver to his house?
7. Who ate a midday meal with the farmer?
8. What animals did Gulliver see in the farmer's house?
9. How did Gulliver kill the rat?
10. Why did Gulliver's dream make him sad?

Chapter 2
1. How old was the farmer's daughter?
2. What was made into a bedroom for Gulliver?
3. What did people think Gulliver was at first?
4. Why did Gulliver laugh at the farmer's friend?
5. Why did the farmer's daughter begin to cry?
6. How did the farmer take his daughter and Gulliver to the town?
7. What made Gulliver feel so tired?
8. Why did the farmer decide to visit all big cities?
9. How far did they all travel each day?
10. How did Gulliver's 'nurse' teach him to read?

Chapter 3   1. Why did Gulliver's health change so much?
2. Who asked to see him at the palace?
3. How much money did the farmer charge for Gulliver?
4. What did the King call Gulliver at first?
5. How did the King prove that Gulliver's story was true?
6. What did his new bedroom look like?
7. Why did Gulliver feel angry with some words of the King?
8. How many daughters had the Queen?
9. What did the dwarf do to Gulliver?
10. What happened to the dwarf afterwards?

Chapter 4   1. Where did Gulliver think that Brobdingnag could be found on the map?
2. Was Brobdingnag an island?
3. Why didn't the people there sell goods to the rest of the world?
4. Where did the people catch their fish?
5. How did Gulliver manage to travel round the country?
6. How could he travel on horseback?
7. How did he see the countryside?
8. What furniture did he have?
9. Why did the chief temple disappoint Gulliver?
10. How many horses were there in the King's guard?

Chapter 5   1. Why did the dwarf shake an apple tree?
2. Why wasn't Gulliver hurt when the dog carried him away?
3. How did Gulliver cut his leg?
4. What did the ladies use to blow him along in his boat?

5. How did the monkey get in Gulliver's room?
6. Why didn't he hide under his bed?
7. Why did people laugh even though Gulliver was in great danger on the roof?
8. Why did the King laugh afterwards at Gulliver and the monkey?
9. Are there many monkeys in Europe?
10. Why did Gulliver fall in the pool of muddy water?

Chapter 6

1. Why did the King of Brobdingnag give orders for any ships that sailed near his coasts to be pulled to the shore?
2. Why was Gulliver always afraid in this country?
3. Why did he decide to take a rest when he was taken to the seashore?
4. What made him wake up suddenly?
5. What did he think was going to happen to him?
6. What difficulties did Gulliver now face?
7. Why did the sailors think that he was a little mad?
8. Why did the captain think that Gulliver had been put in the box?
9. Why did Gulliver think he was still in Lilliput even after he landed in England?
10. Why did Gulliver think he would not write any books?

OXFORD PROGRESSIVE ENGLISH READERS

GRADE 1
Vocabulary restricted to 1900 head words
Illustrations in both full colour and two colours
One illustration for every 6 pages on average

Don Quixote	CERVANTES
Great Expectations	CHARLES DICKENS
Gulliver's Travels	JONATHAN SWIFT
Jane Eyre	CHARLOTTE BRONTE
Little Women	LOUISA M. ALCOTT
Oliver Twist	CHARLES DICKENS
Stories of Shakespeare's Plays I	RETOLD BY N. KATES
Tales from Tolstoy	RETOLD BY R.D. BINFIELD
The Tale of the Bounty	RETOLD BY H.G. WYATT
The Tiger of Lembah Pahit	NORMA R. YOUNGBERG
The Stone Junk	RETOLD BY D.H. HOWE
Treasure Island	R.L. STEVENSON

GRADE 2
Vocabulary restricted to 2900 head words
One two-coloured illustration every 10 pages on average

A Tale of Two Cities	CHARLES DICKENS
Beau Geste	P.C. WREN
David Copperfield	CHARLES DICKENS
Robinson Crusoe	DANIEL DEFOE
Seven Chinese Stories	T.J. SHERIDAN
Stories of Shakespeare's Plays II	RETOLD BY WYATT AND FULLERTON
The Crocodile Dies Twice	SHAMUS FRAZER
The Hound of the Baskervilles	SIR ARTHUR CONAN DOYLE

GRADE 3
Vocabulary restricted to 3500 head words
One two-coloured illustration every 15 pages on average

Lady Precious Stream	S.I. HSIUNG
Seven Stories	H.G. WELLS
Stories of Shakespeare's Plays III	RETOLD BY H.G. WYATT
The Moonstone	WILKIE COLLINS
The Red Winds	SHAMUS FRAZER
The War of the Worlds	H.G. WELLS

60p net.